Toys, Gifts & Decorations

Toys, Gifts & Decorations

Leila Aitken

ILLUSTRATIONS BY GLEN CRAIG

DRYAD PRESS LTD

London

This book is for those who find positive pleasure in a creative hobby, and for my family, especially Bobby.

ISBN 0 8521 9611 3

Typeset by Tek-Art Ltd, Kent
and printed in Great Britain by
Anchor Brendon Ltd
Tiptree, Essex
for the publishers
Dryad Press Ltd
4 Fitzhardinge Street
London W1H 0AH

Contents

Soft Toys

Percy, Pete and Bob

1 Furry Rabbits

This is a delightful family of furry rabbits. The largest rabbit, Percy, is 90cm high from the tip of his ears to his tail, the medium sized rabbit, Pete, is 40cm high and Bob, the small rabbit is 30cm. They are all made from long-pile fur fabric with an underbody and ear linings of a flowery cotton fabric.

Percy is an ideal size for an older child or teenager. Make the underbody of the rabbit from the same fabric as the curtains or quilt cover to stand in the corner of their room as a decorative toy. Pete is a soft and cuddly toy for any age, and Bob is an ideal pram toy for a small baby.

All the rabbits are easy and quick to make. They are made from only three pattern pieces, which are such simple shapes that they are very easy to copy from the grid pattern (diagram 1). If you haven't used a grid pattern before, this is a good one on which to start. Make the three different sizes of rabbit by varying the size of the squares of the grid on which you copy the outline from the pattern diagram.

The eyes used for the rabbits are the plastic safety-lock type. These are very realistic and can be bought from craft shops or the trimmings counter of large stores. They consist of a plastic eye front (which looks like glass) and a metal washer which is pushed very tightly on to the shank of the eye on the inside of the toy, making it impossible for a child to prise the eye loose.

PERCY – LARGE RABBIT

Making the pattern for the rabbit

Mark a sheet of plain paper, measuring 40cm × 120cm into 10cm squares. Copy the outline on the squares shown in our pattern diagram on to the squares marked on your paper so that the outline in each square corresponds exactly. Mark the fold on the underbody, positions A and B, and the position for the eye. Cut out the pattern.

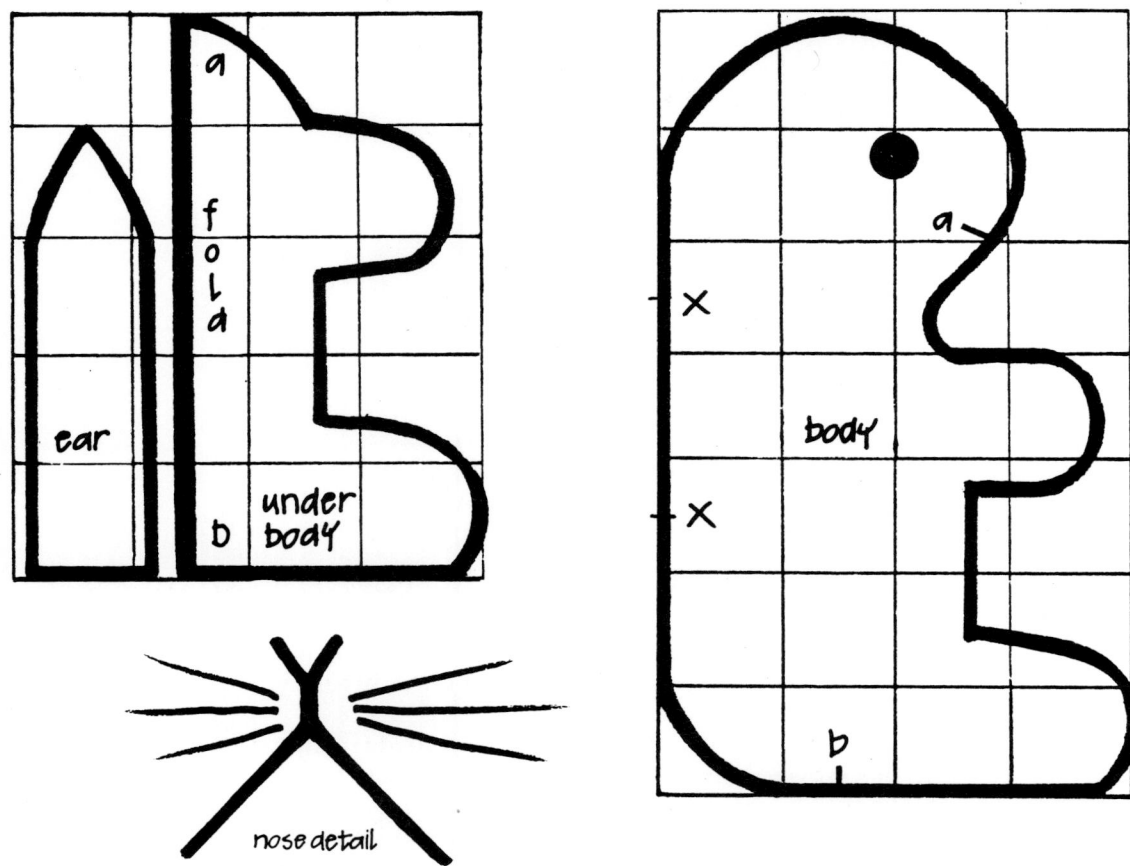

Diagram 1 Rabbit pattern

Large rabbit
   1 square = 10cm
Medium rabbit
   1 square = 5cm
Small rabbit
   1 square = 3cm

Materials required

PETE – MEDIUM RABBIT
Mark a sheet of plain paper measuring 20cm × 60cm into 5cm squares. Follow the instructions as above.

BOB – SMALL RABBIT
Mark a sheet of plain paper measuring 36cm × 12cm into 3cm squares. Follow the instructions as above.

LARGE RABBIT
70cm long-pile fur fabric, at least 120cm wide.
50cm cotton fabric, 90cm wide
1.5 kg polyester filling
1 pair eyes (large)
Scrap black wool
2 lengths soft wire 80cm long

MEDIUM RABBIT
40cm long-pile fur fabric, at least 90cm wide.
30cm cotton fabric, 90cm wide
250g polyester filling
1 pair eyes (medium)
Scrap black wool
2 lengths soft wire 40cm long

SMALL RABBIT
The small rabbit can be made from scraps left over from the other rabbits. If you are only making the small rabbit, you will need to buy:
30cm of long-pile fur fabric
20cm cotton fabric
100g polyester filling
1 pair eyes (small)
Scrap black wool

Cutting out (all sizes)

Seam turnings are not allowed on the pattern. Allow 6mm turnings throughout. When cutting out the fur fabric the pile of the fur should run downwards. Cut the backing of the fur fabric with the point of the scissors only to avoid cutting the pile. Cut two body pieces and two ear pieces in fur fabric. Remember to reverse the pattern for one body piece. Cut a circle of fur fabric 20cm diameter (large rabbit), 15cm diameter (medium rabbit) and 10cm diameter (small rabbit) for the tail.

Cut out the underbody in cotton fabric with the edge AB, against the fold of the fabric. Cut two ear pieces in cotton fabric.

Mark positions A and B on the body and underbody pieces and the position for the eye.

Construction

SEWING INSTRUCTIONS (all sizes)
Take 6mm seams throughout. Stitch the body pieces together, round the curve of the head and down the back, between A and B (diagram 2). Leave open between X and X for stuffing. With right sides facing, join the underbody to the body matching A to A, B to B and paws and feet. Turn right side out through the opening.

Eyes
Snip the fabric at the position marked for the eye. Insert the shank of the eye through the fur fabric from the right side. Press the safety washer firmly down on to the shank of the eye, inside the toy (diagram 3).

Stuff the body firmly, packing the stuffing well into the paws and feet in small amounts. Oversew the opening together.

Diagram 2 Seams

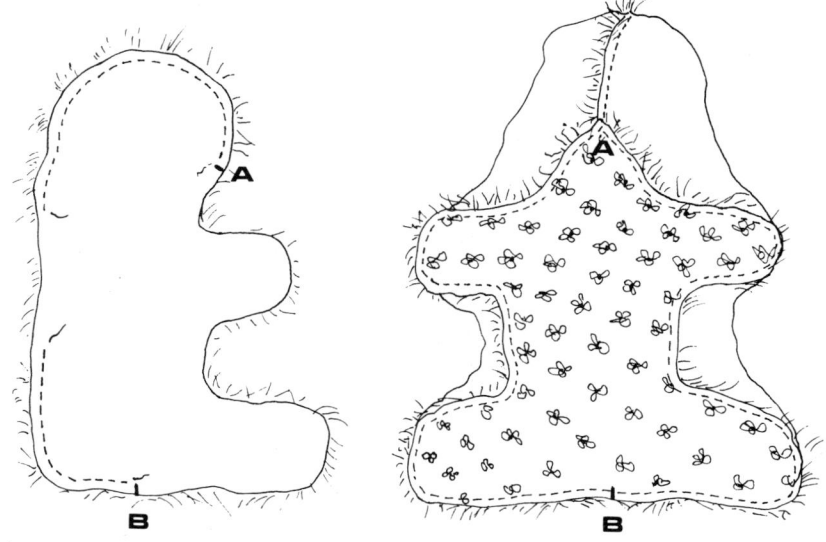

Ears

Match a fur fabric ear piece to a cotton ear piece and with right sides facing, stitch round the two long sides. Turn right side out (diagram 3).

Bend a length of wire in half. Turn up the ends, to form a small loop. Wrap the wire in bias binding (diagram 3). Insert the wire into the ear. Stitch the loops of wire to the seam turnings at the base of the ear. Stab stitch invisibly through the fur to hold the wire against the seam turnings at the sides of the ear. Stitch the ears securely to the back of the head.

Note: The small rabbit does not need wired ears.

Nose

Embroider the nose detail in thick black wool, as illustrated.

*Diagram 3
Construction of the
features*

Tail

Run a gathering thread around the outside of the circle of fur fabric. Add a little stuffing in the centre and draw up the gathering thread to form a round tail (diagram 3). Stitch securely to the back of the rabbit at the base.

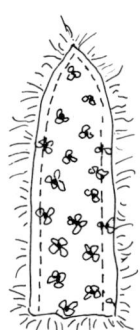
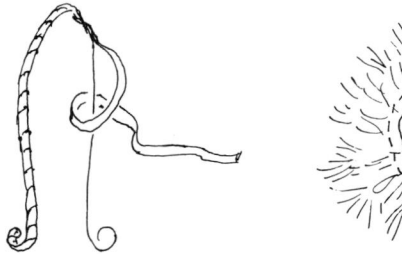
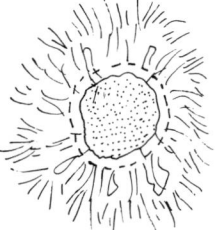

2 Winston the Bulldog

Winston the bulldog is a toy for all ages and is sure to become a family favourite. He would also make an amusing gift for a dog-lover living in a flat or in the city.

Winston is very realistic, made in a creamy-beige furnishing velvet with dark brown markings and is 22cm high and 42cm long. He has a wet-look plastic nose and glass eyes which are readily available at craft shops or the haberdashery counters of large stores. *Diagram 4*

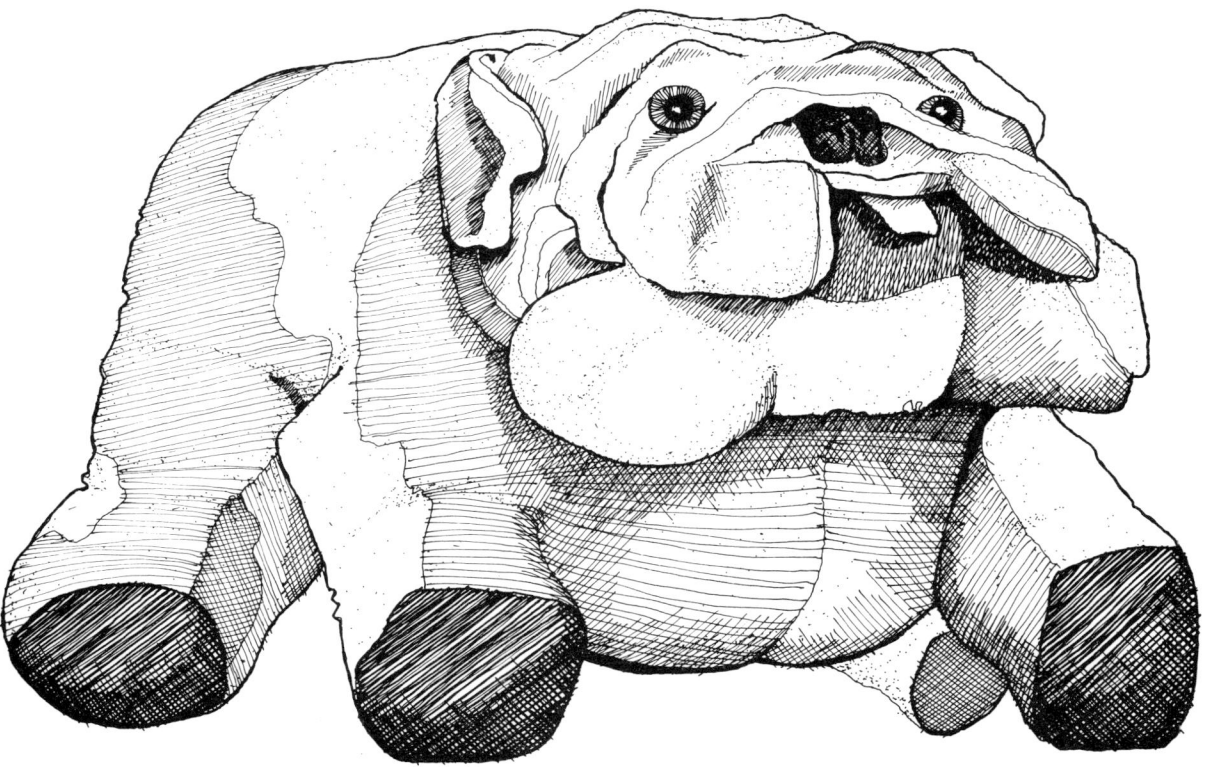

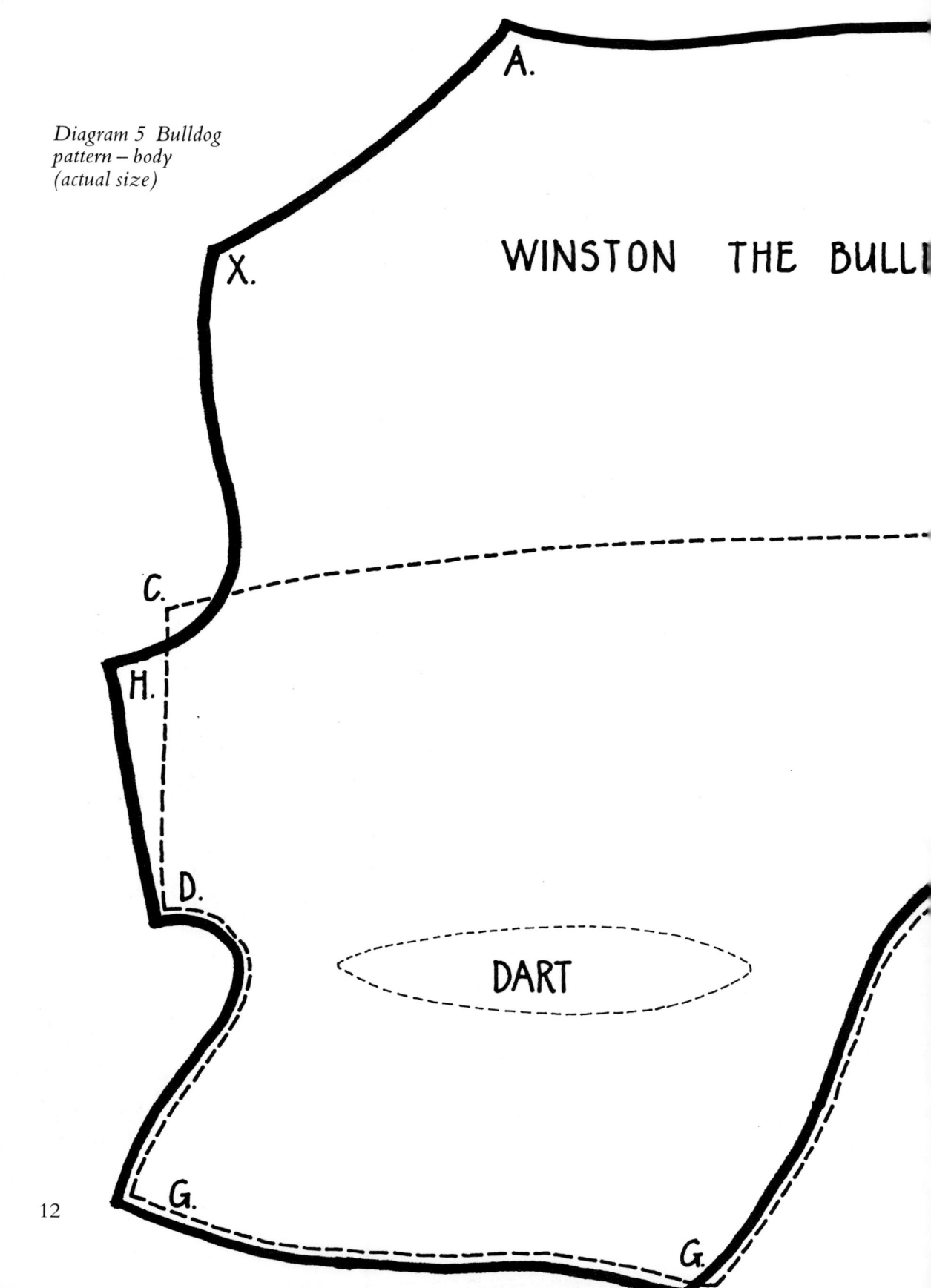

*Diagram 5 Bulldog
pattern – body
(actual size)*

A.

X.

WINSTON   THE   BULL

C.

H.

D.

DART

G.

G.

12

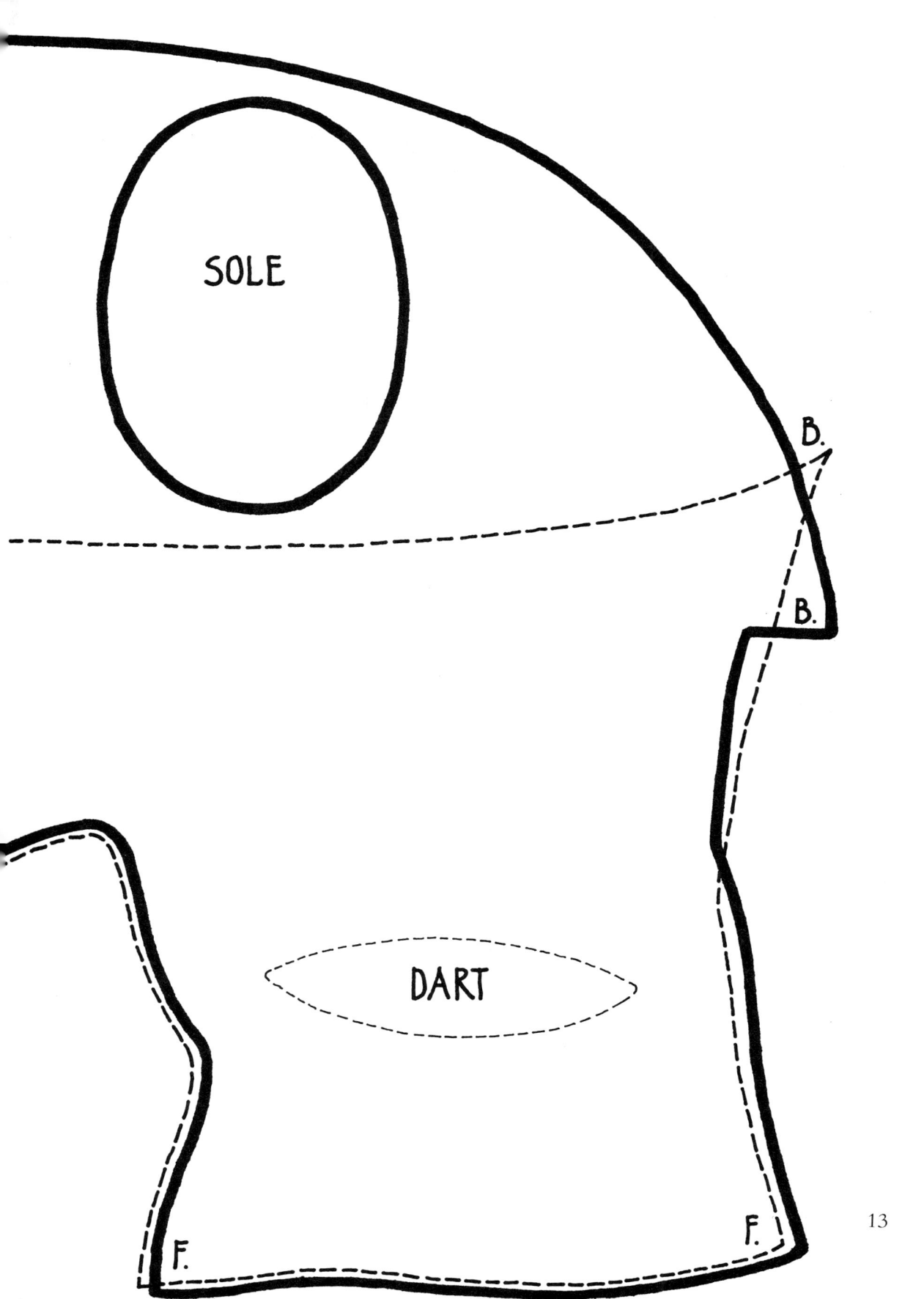

SOLE

B.

B.

DART

F.

F.

13

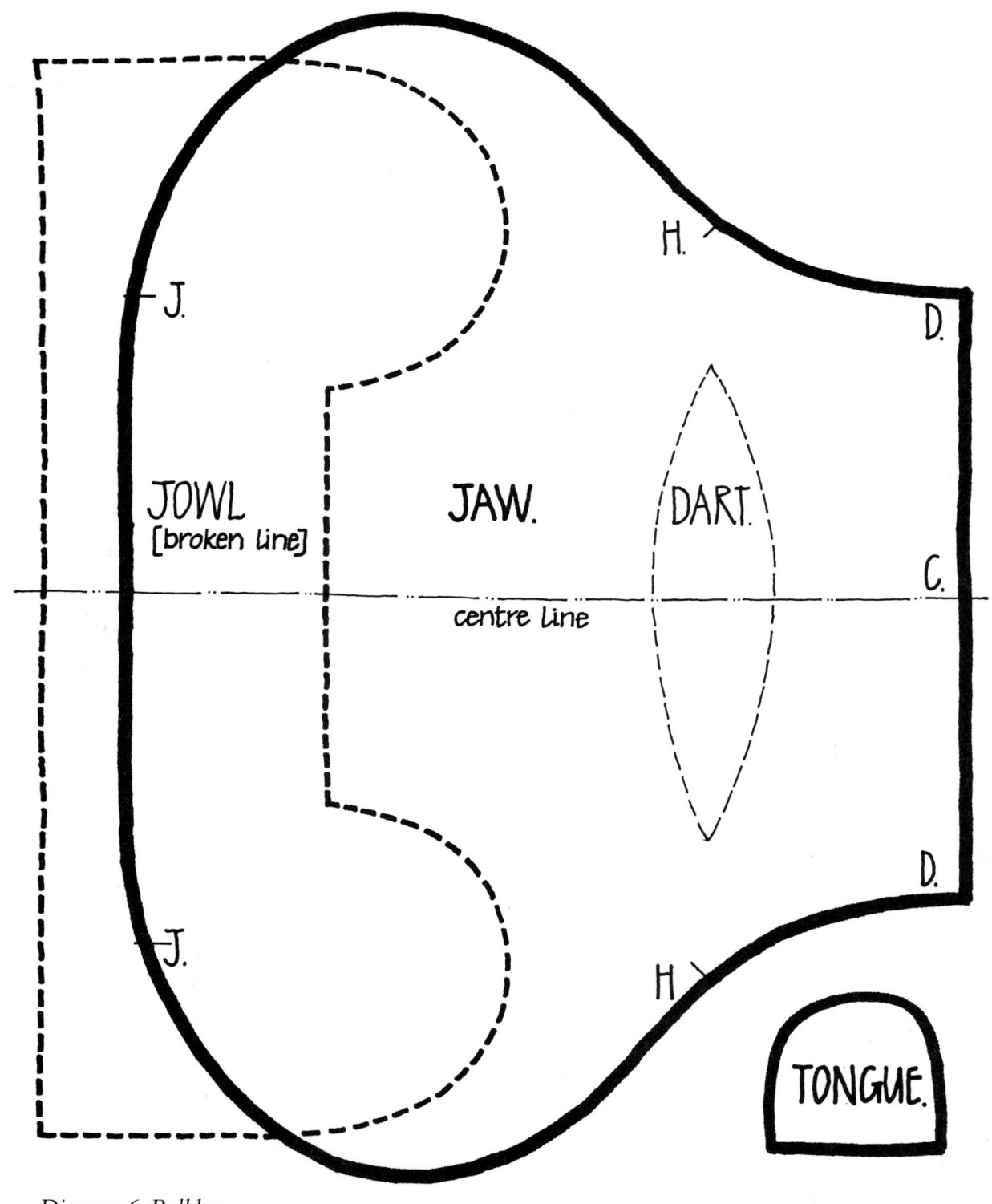

J.

H.

D.

JOWL
[broken line]

JAW.

DART.

C.

centre line

J.

D.

H

TONGUE.

*Diagram 6 Bulldog
pattern – tongue, jaws
and jowel (actual size)*

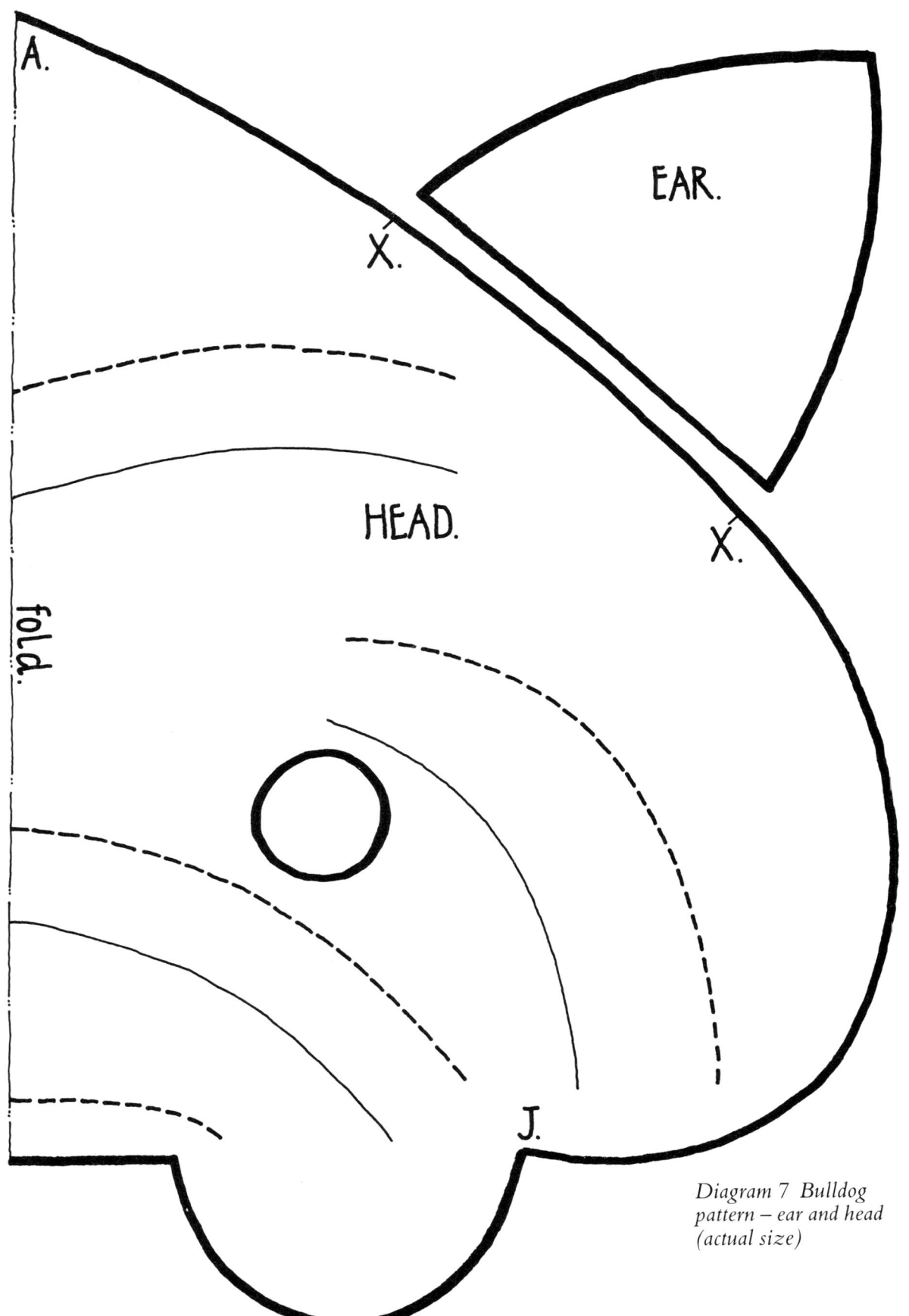

A.

EAR.

X.

X.

HEAD.

fold

J.

Diagram 7 Bulldog pattern – ear and head (actual size)

Making the bulldog pattern

Trace the pattern pieces given (diagrams 5, 6 and 7), and cut out these shapes. Mark all the letters accurately and the position of the darts on the jaw and underbody. (There are no darts on the body pieces.) Mark the solid and dotted lines on the head, and the position for the nose and eyes.

Materials required

60cm furnishing velvet, 122cm wide
10cm dark brown furnishing velvet
Scrap red felt
Piece polyester wadding, 25cm × 35cm
1 pair large glass eyes
A narrow dog collar, 40cm long
500g polyester filling
Brown cold-water fabric dye

Cutting out

Place the pattern pieces following the cutting layout (diagram 8) with the pile of the velvet running down on the body and head as indicated by the arrow and across on the underbody. Allow 6mm

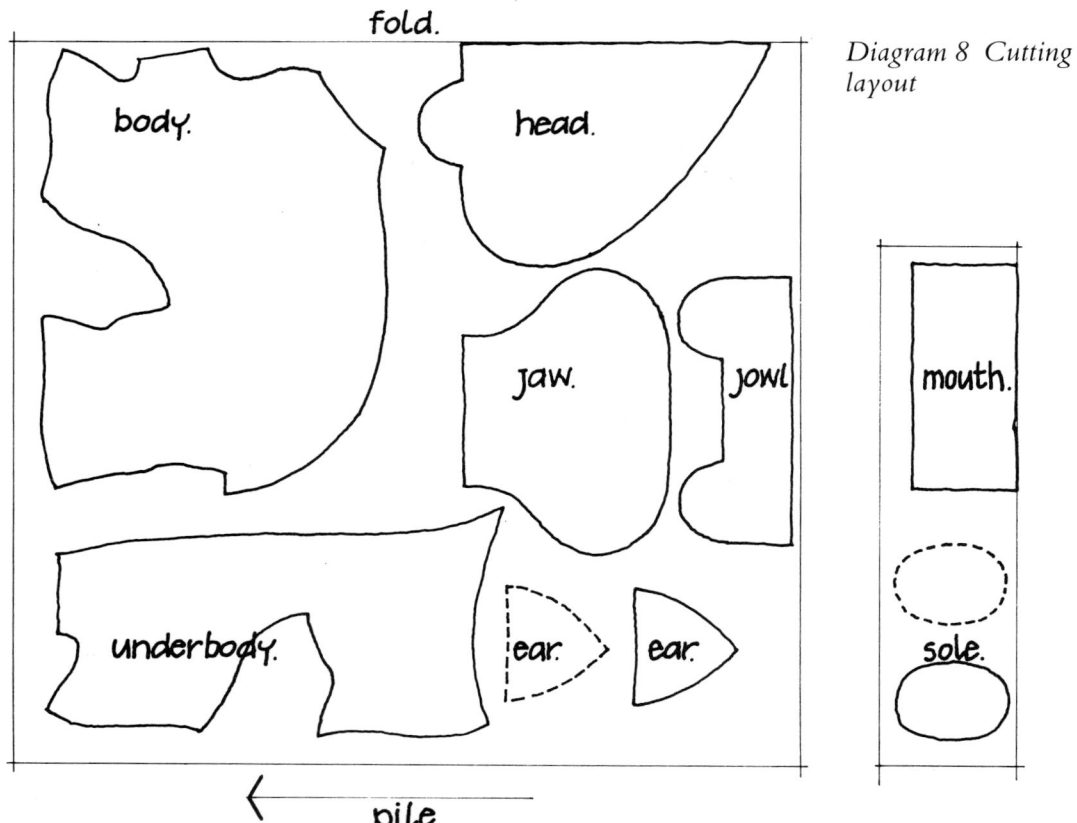

Diagram 8 Cutting layout

turnings. In beige velvet, cut out two body pieces, two underbody pieces, four ears and one head, placing the head pattern to the fold as marked. Cut one jaw and one jowl piece. In dark brown velvet cut four sole pieces and a strip 6cm × 15cm for the mouth. Cut the tongue from a scrap of red felt.

Mark the solid and dotted lines on the head, with thread. Mark the darts and pencil the position of the letters on the inside of the fabric. This will make joining up the pieces very simple.

SEWING INSTRUCTIONS (diagram 9)

Construction

Stitch the body pieces, right sides together, along the top edge AB (diagram 9a). Stitch the long side of the underbody BC (diagram 9b). Stitch the jaw to the underbody, joining DCD. Stitch the dart in the jaw (diagram 9c). Stitch the small darts in the underbody.

Place the underbody on top of the body, with right sides facing. Stitch the outside edges matching H and D, the feet at G and F and the tail at B. Leave the soles of the feet open (diagram 9d).

Diagram 9

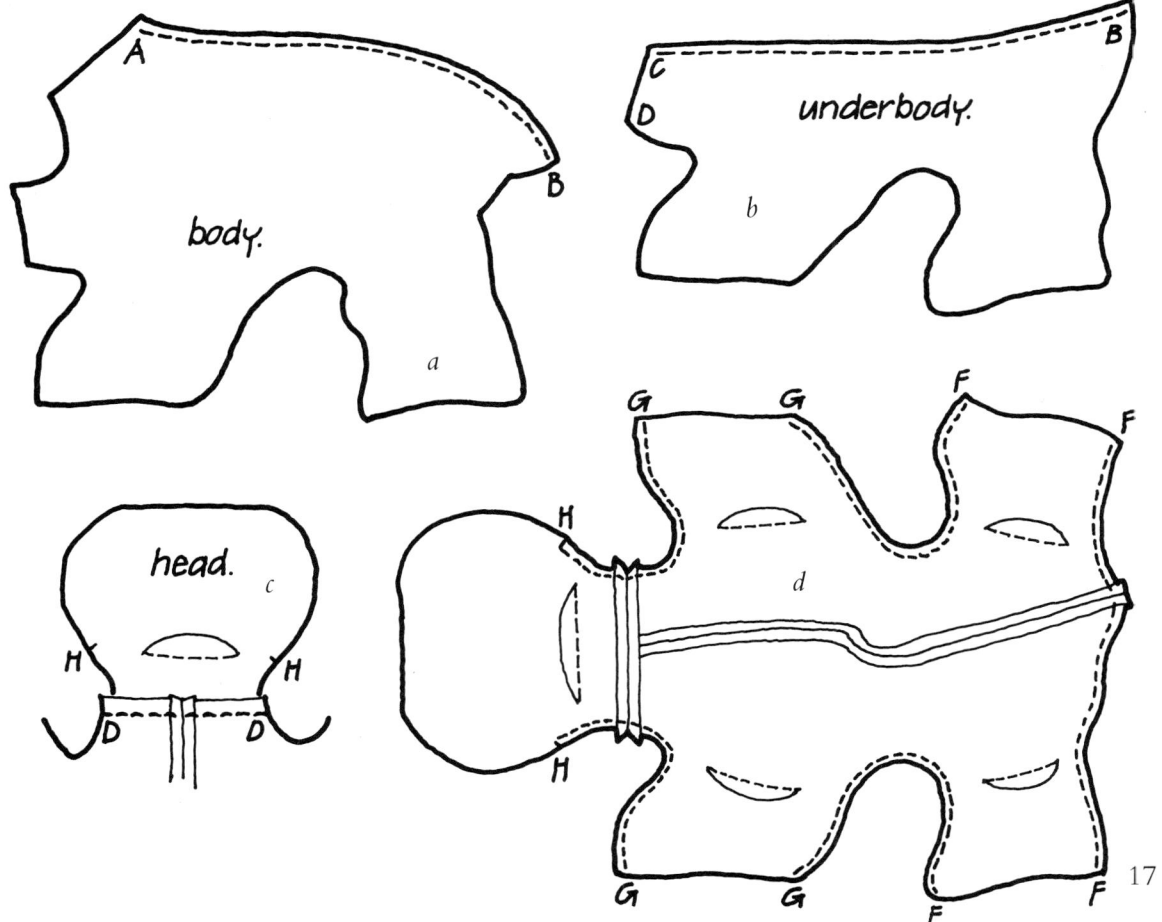

17

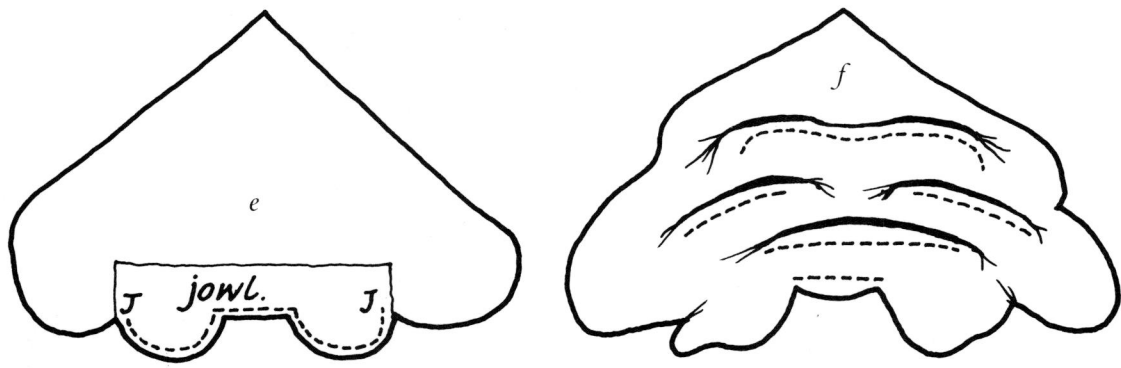

Diagram 9 (continued)

Furrows

Cut a piece of wadding the same shape as the head pattern. Tack the wadding to the wrong side of the head piece, round the outside edges. Place the jowl piece right sides together on top of the jowl shape on the head matching J and J. Stitch round the curves between J and J (diagram 9e). Clip the seam turnings. Turn the jowl to the inside.

Push a little polyester filling into the curves of the jowls and along the seam line. Using an invisible stab stitch, stitch along the dotted line below the nose through all thicknesses.

Bring the solid and the dotted line above the nose together, enclosing the wadding and the raw edge of the jowl piece, to form a tuck. Stab stitch through all thicknesses along the lines.

Bring the solid and the dotted line above each eye together. Stab stitch together through all thicknesses. Stitch the wavy, dotted and solid lines on the forehead together in the same way (diagram 9f).

Nose and eyes

Pierce the fabric and wadding in the centre of the spot marked for the nose, using the point of the scissors. Push the shank of the nose through all the thicknesses from the right side. Press the safety washer firmly on to the shank on the wrong side of the fabric (diagram 10a).

Insert the eyes in the same way. Put a stitch or two in the tuck above the eye so that it folds downwards, slightly covering the edge of the eye.

Ears

Stitch the ears in pairs, right sides together round the curved sides. Leave the straight side open (diagram 10b). Turn right side out. Tack the open edges together.

Tack the ears to the head with the open edge between XX, and the point of the ear lying towards the eye.

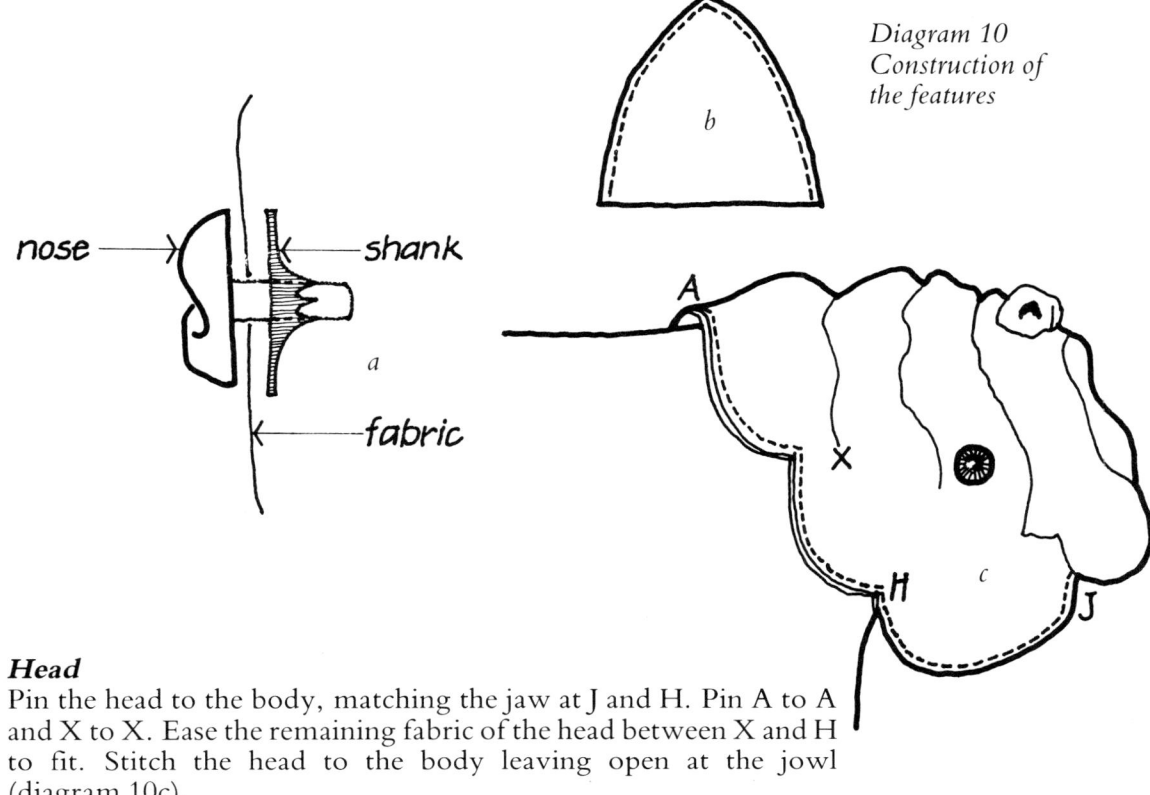

*Diagram 10
Construction of
the features*

nose ———> ⊢—— shank

a

⊢———fabric

Head
Pin the head to the body, matching the jaw at J and H. Pin A to A
and X to X. Ease the remaining fabric of the head between X and H
to fit. Stitch the head to the body leaving open at the jowl
(diagram 10c).

Feet
Open out the feet and insert the sole pieces, right sides inside. Ease
to fit and stitch round the outside edges.

Turn the toy right side out through the mouth.

Stuffing
Pack in the stuffing through the mouth, adding the stuffing in small
quantities, to keep the shape of the toy. Stuff the feet and legs first,
then the body. Pack the filling into the jowls and cheeks and then
complete the stuffing of the head. To give the head and cheeks the
bulges you want, insert a long darning needle into the fabric and
tease the stuffing where it is needed with the point of the needle.
Stitch the point of the ears to the side of the head.

Mouth
By hand, stitch the straight edge of the tongue inside the mouth to
the line of stitching below the nose. Stitch the brown velvet strip,
right sides together to the open edge of the jaw (diagram 10d). Turn

Diagram 10
(continued)

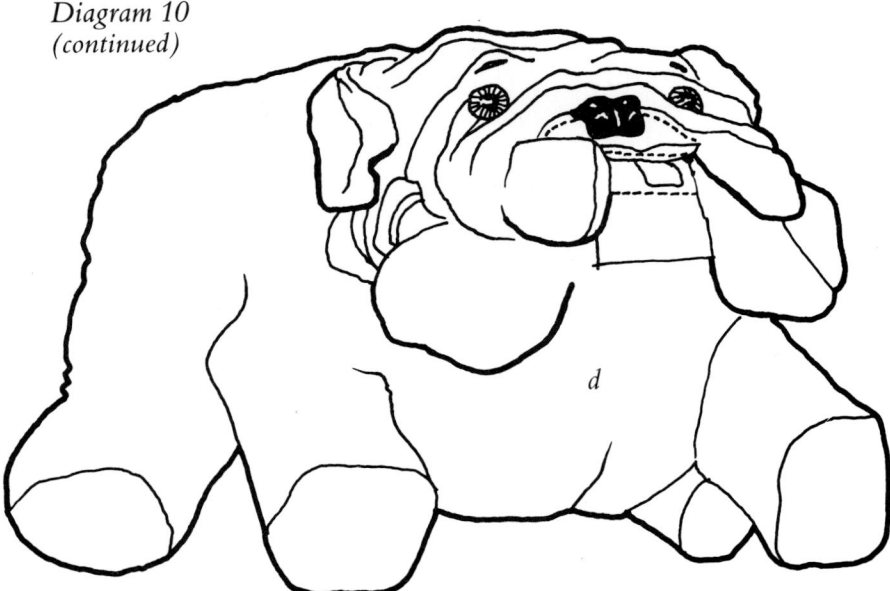

the strip upwards closing the opening and hem the underside of the mouth and jowls to the velvet where they meet.

Markings

Make up the dye according to the instructions. Pencil the outline to be dyed. Mark an irregular shape over the right shoulder down to the eye, and an irregular outline over the left hind leg, and up the left side of the body. Paint these outlines with the dye using a stiff paint–brush or an old toothbrush.

Finally, put on the collar, pulling in the dog's neck to fit. With the point of a long needle, tease the stuffing towards the collar to form bulges, rather than wrinkles, each side of the collar.

3 Soft & Simple Dolls

Diagram 11

Everyone loves rag dolls. They are especially popular with young children as they are the cuddliest of all dolls (diagram 23).

Stockinet is the ideal material for a rag doll. It makes a very soft squashy doll and the fabric can be moulded into appealing features. These two delightful dolls are made from good quality stockinet, filled with washable polyester filling. The smaller doll, Fat Harriet, is 40cm tall and the long, lanky doll, Skinny Lizzy, is 50cm tall. They are both made from this basic pattern and are very simple to make.

The chubby cheeks are formed by adding extra bulges of filling to the head and stretching a circle of stockinet over the top to cover it. You can add dimples, worry lines or a snub nose to give a definite shape and expression to the face, and as no two stockinet dolls turn out the same, they are great fun to make.

It is very important to use good quality tubular stockinet for these dolls – not the dish cloth variety. It should be closely knitted and you can buy it from craft shops or doll-maker's suppliers.

Addresses of suppliers are listed at the end of the book.

Making the rag doll pattern

Trace the pattern pieces given here (diagrams 12, 13 and 14), and cut out these shapes. Mark the position of the letters and the arrows. To make the pattern for Skinny Lizzy, lengthen the body piece at E by 2.5cm, the top of the leg by 8cm, and the arm piece at CD by 5cm.

Materials required

FAT HARRIET
35cm good quality cream stockinet 140cm wide
Scrap black stockinet, or calico
150g polyester filling
Scrap black felt
Glue
Dolls' hair, or old wig (brown)
15cm narrow tape
Hair ribbon

SKINNY LIZZY
40cm good quality cream stockinet 140cm wide
Scrap black stockinet, or calico
250g polyester filling
Scrap blue felt
Glue
Dolls' hair, or old wig (fair)
15cm narrow tape
Hair ribbon

Diagram 12 Doll pattern – bodice, sleeve and pants (actual size)

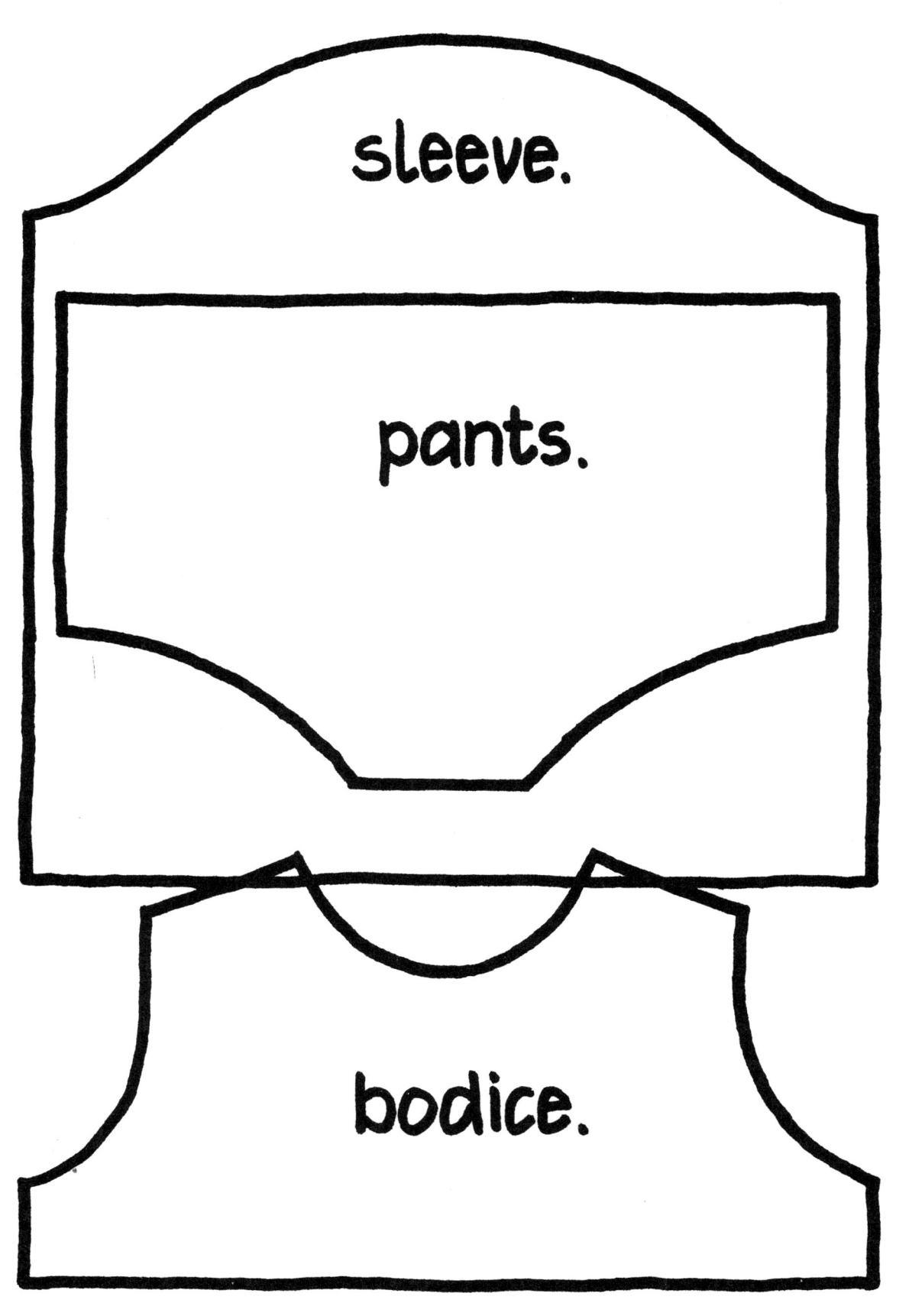

sleeve.

pants.

bodice.

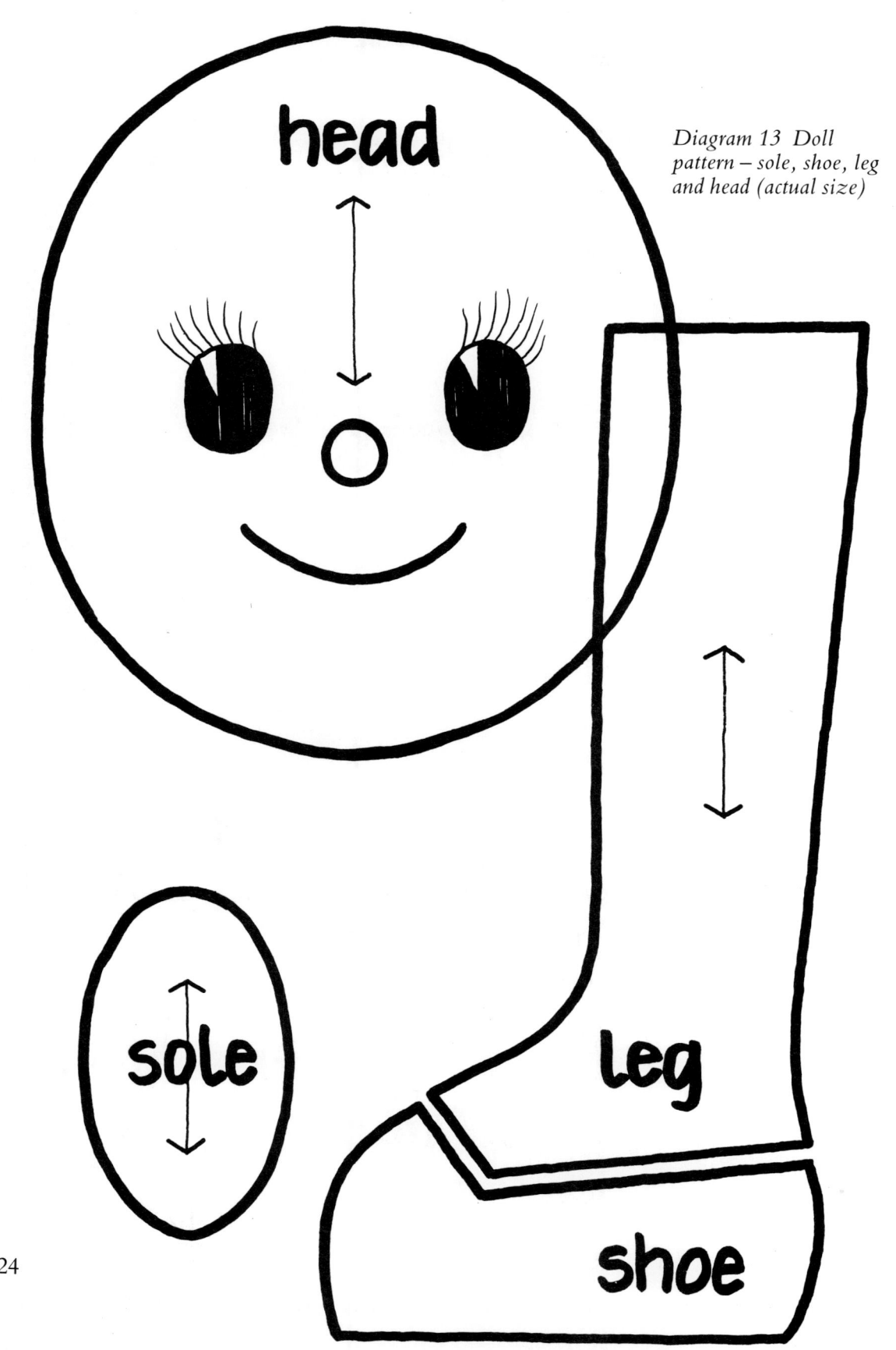

head

Diagram 13 Doll
pattern – sole, shoe, leg
and head (actual size)

sole

leg

shoe

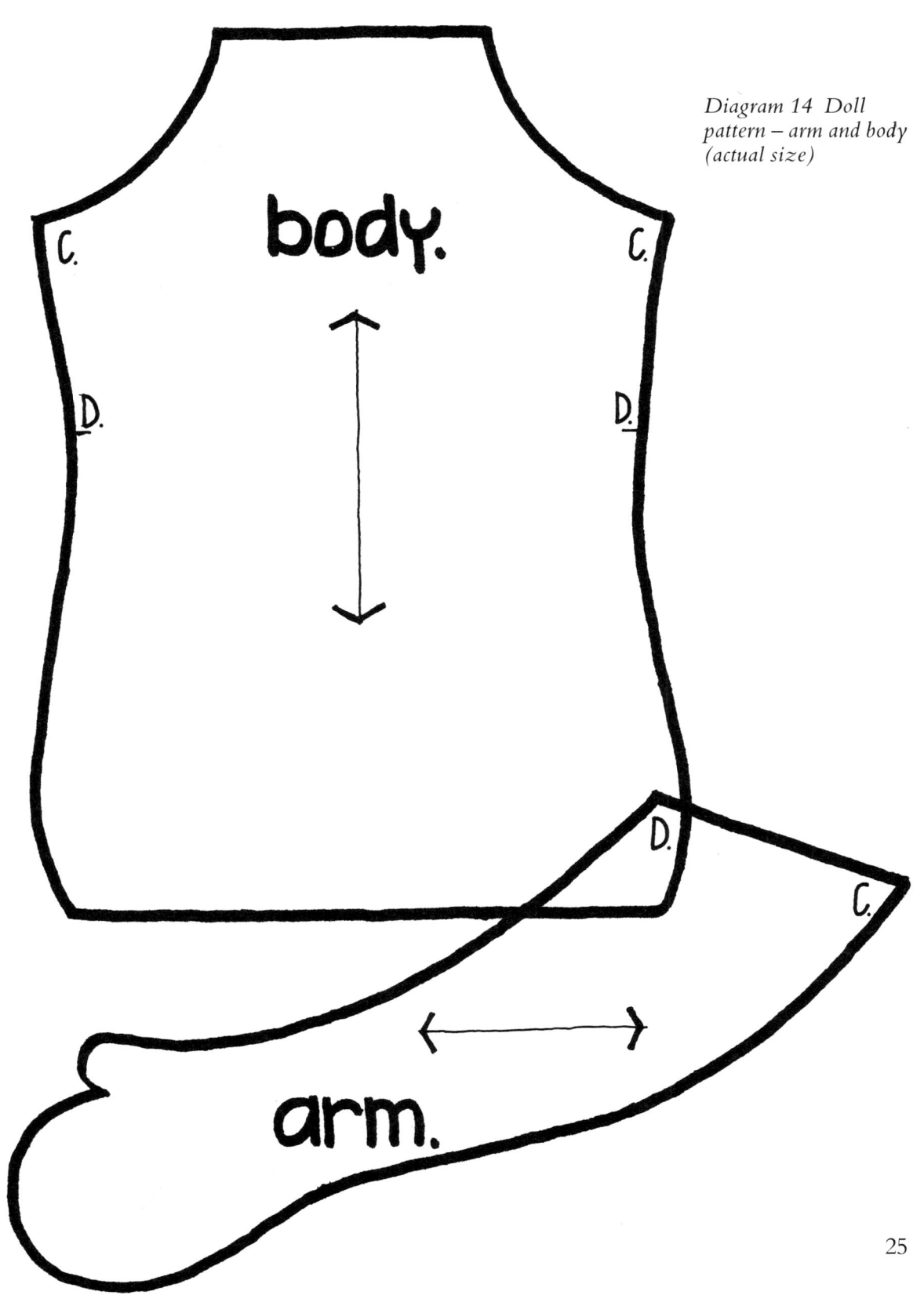

Diagram 14 Doll pattern – arm and body (actual size)

body.

C.

C.

D.

D.

D.

C.

arm.

Cutting out both dolls

No turnings are allowed on the pattern (diagram 15). Allow 6mm turnings throughout. Place the pattern pieces following the cutting layout given, with the arrows in the direction shown, so that the maximum stretch of the fabric is round the body of the doll. Cut one 20cm diameter circle for the face. From the remaining fabric cut a 3cm diameter circle for the nose, two 5cm diameter circles for the cheeks and a 4cm diameter circle for the chin. Cut four shoe pieces and two sole pieces in black fabric.

Construction

SEWING INSTRUCTIONS (both dolls)

Stockinet is easier to sew by hand, using a close back stitch, but it can be machined using a long machine stitch and releasing the pressure knob on the machine a little. On difficult curves lift the presser foot and ease the fabric round. Take 6mm seams throughout.

Legs

Join the shoe to the leg, matching A to A and B to B. Stitch the legs together in pairs, leaving an opening of about 4cm at the back of the leg for stuffing. Leave open at the top of the leg and the sole. Stitch the sole to the shoe. Turn legs right side out. Cut two sole pieces in thin card. Slip these inside the feet.

Arms

Stitch the arms together in pairs, leaving the top open and an opening of about 4cm in one seam. Turn right side out.

Body

Tack across the top of the legs so that the seams lie on top of each other. With the right side of the body piece uppermost, place the legs on the body, raw edges together, each side of E (diagram 16a). Tack across the base. Fold up the legs and pin to the centre of the body. (This is to keep them away from the stitching line.)

Pin the arms to the body, raw edges together, matching C and D. Tack the edges (diagram 16b). Place the other body piece on top of the first, wrong side uppermost, enclosing the arms and legs. Stitch round the outer edges, leaving open at the neck edge (diagram 16c). Turn right side out through the opening. Release the arms and legs.

Stuff the body, arms and legs. Pack the stuffing in gradually, using small amounts to avoid a lumpy effect and over-stretching the stockinet. Oversew the openings in the arms and legs.

Cut a strip of black stockinet 9cm × 2cm. Fold it in three lengthways to conceal the raw edges and stitch this strap to the inside of the shoe, stretch it over the foot and stitch to the outside of the shoe.

Diagram 15 Cutting layout

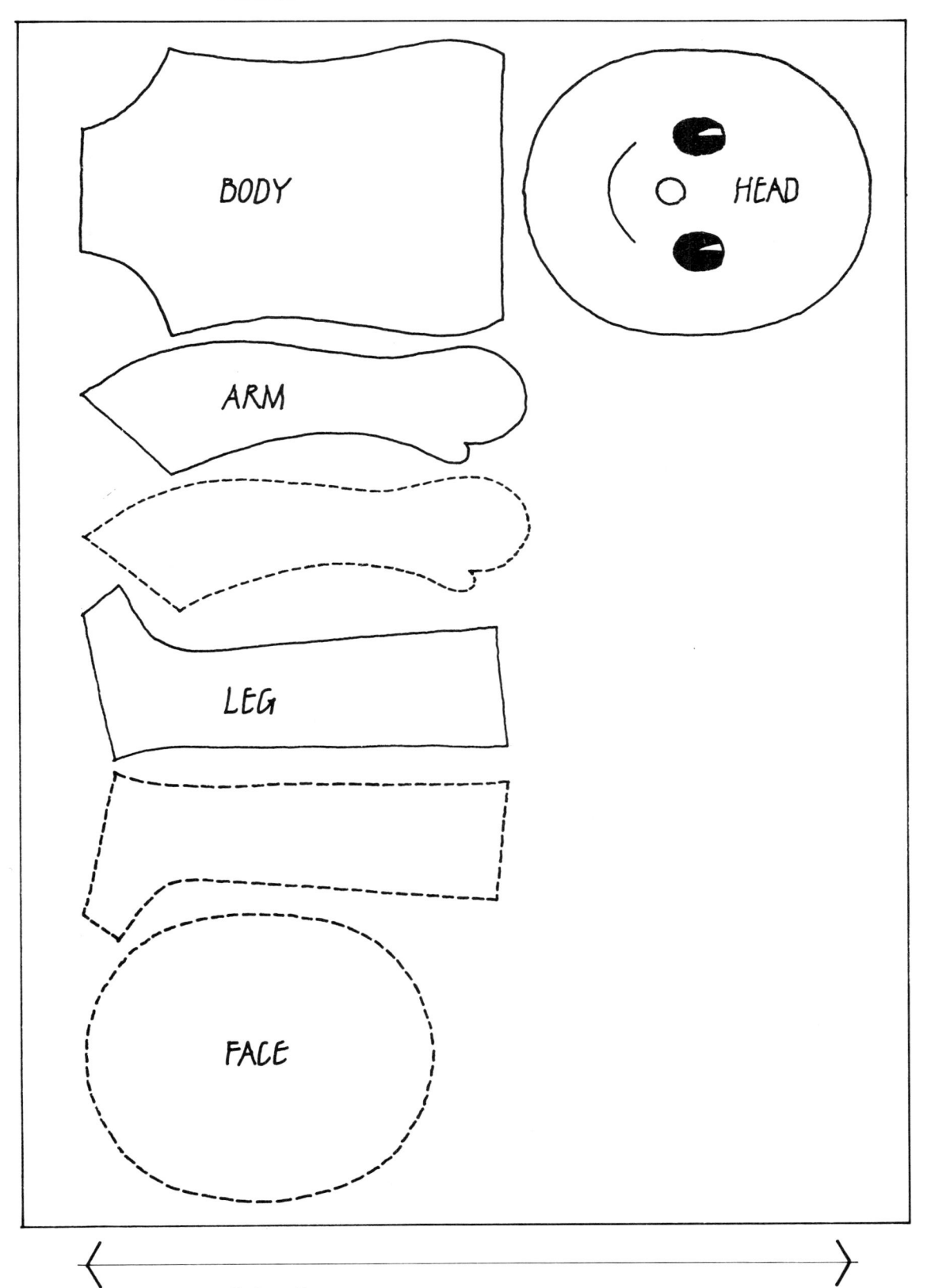

BODY

HEAD

ARM

LEG

FACE

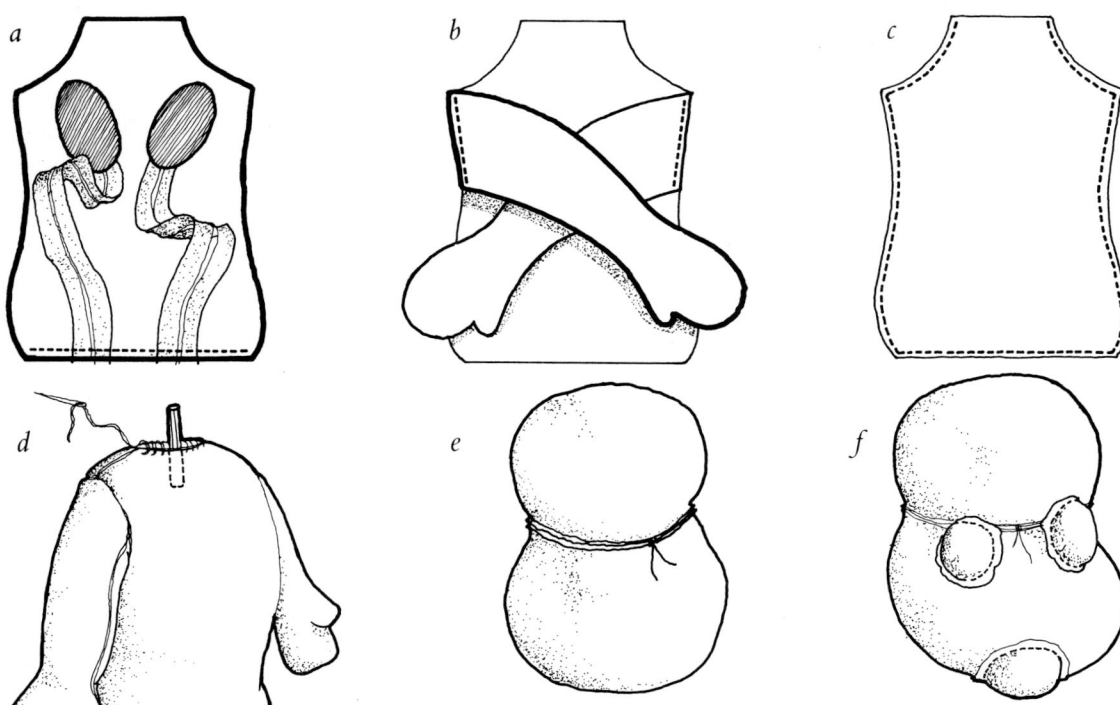

Diagram 16

Push a piece of thin dowelling or a pencil about 12cm long into the neck half-way down into the centre of the body stuffing. Leave the other half protruding and oversew the neck opening together (diagram 16d).

Head
Stitch the two head pieces together round the outside edges, leaving an opening for stuffing. Turn inside out through the opening. Stuff into a smooth oval shape and oversew the opening together.

Features
Tie a length of strong thread round the head, drawing in the fullness to create the forehead and eye-line (diagram 16e). Run a gathering thread round the outside of the circles cut for the cheeks and chin. Place a small pad of stuffing in the centre of the circle, draw up the gathering stitches a little and stitch the cheek and chin pieces to the face with running stitches (diagram 16f).

Run a gathering thread around the edge of the face piece. Smooth it over the cheeks, chin and the head and draw up the thread at the back of the head. Sew the edges of the fabric together with long threads at the back of the head (diagram 17a). Smooth the creases from the chin and cheeks. (The other creases and the untidy threads will be covered by the neck and mob cap.)

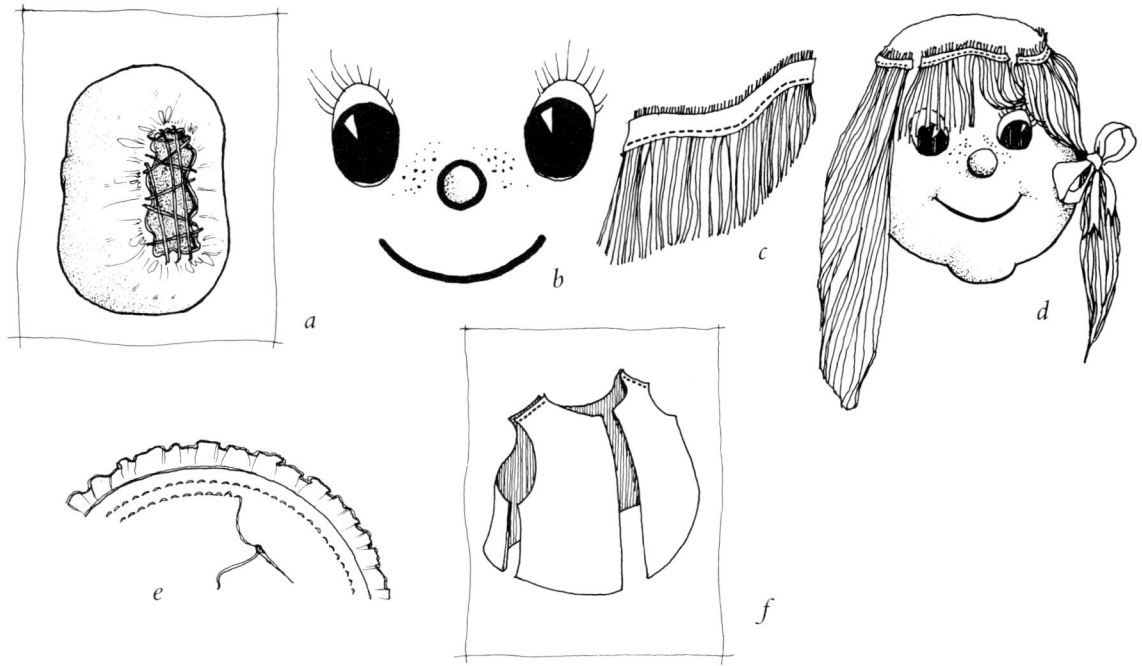

Thread a long needle with a double thread. Make one stitch into each eye socket from the back of the head, through the stuffing and pull the thread taut. Cut two oval shapes in black felt for the eyes, and a slightly larger oval of white felt (diagram 17b). Glue in place as shown. Draw in lashes in black felt pen.

Run a gathering thread around the small circle cut for the nose. Roll a tiny piece of stuffing into a ball, cover with the stockinet. Draw up the gathering thread tightly and stitch this ball in place for the nose.

Embroider a small curve in red thread between the nose and chin for the mouth. At each side of the mouth between the mouth and the cheeks, take a small stitch from the back of the head to pull the fabric taut and form dimples.

Brush the cheeks and chin with pink powder blusher. Add a small dab of white paint to the eye, to give a highlight effect. (Typists' liquid paper is ideal for this.)

Attaching the head

Position the neck of the doll to the back of the head about 4cm up from the chin. Pin it first to experiment with various positions until you have the most pleasing effect. Fixing the head at an angle for example, gives the doll a very appealing expression.

Snip the fabric where the neck joins the back of the head. Insert

Diagram 17

the rest of the pencil into the head, easing it into the stuffing. Oversew the head and neck together at the back, adding a dab of glue over the stitching. (This will be covered.) Invisibly slip stitch the neck to the underneath of the chin where it touches.

Hair

Cut three lengths of tape 5cm long. Cut strands of hair approximately 7cm long. Stitch and glue one end of these strands to one tape forming a fringe (diagram 17c). Glue and stitch the fringe in place to the front of the head at the top. Cut strands of hair 15cm long and glue and stitch these strands to the other pieces of tape. Glue and stitch these tapes to the sides of the head each side of the fringe (diagram 17d). Smear glue over the sides of the head. Smooth the long hair down over sides of the head. Bunch the hair below the cheeks and tie with ribbon. Trim the fringe and the ends of the hair, use hair spray to hold in place.

Materials required

CLOTHES

Dress, mob cap and pants

50cm floral cotton with a small scale design, 90cm wide (for Skinny Lizzy you will need 60cm)
2m narrow lace
7cm narrow velcro fastening
16cm narrow elastic

Apron and mob cap lining

30cm plain fabric 90cm wide (for Skinny Lizzy you will need 40cm)
1.30m frilled lace
40cm narrow tape
70cm ribbon 1cm wide

Cutting out

Dress, mob cap and pants

Cut a 20cm strip across the full width of the fabric. (For Skinny Lizzy make this strip 30cm.) At one end of the remaining fabric cut a circle 24cm diameter (draw round a dinner plate). From the remaining fabric cut two pants, two bodices and two sleeves. (For Skinny Lizzy lengthen the sleeve pattern 5cm.) Allow 6mm turnings on all pattern pieces.

Apron and mob cap lining

Cut a circle 24cm diameter from one end of the fabric. From the remaining fabric cut a strip 15cm × 60cm (for Skinny Lizzy make this strip 25cm × 60cm) for the skirt of the apron. Cut a strip 25cm × 6cm for the waistband and two strips 15cm × 7cm for the straps.

SEWING INSTRUCTIONS

Mob cap

Pin the mob cap and mob cap lining with right sides together. Stitch round the outer edge, taking a 6mm seam and leaving an opening of approximately 5cm in the stitching. Turn right side out through the opening. Oversew the opening. Stitch some narrow lace round the edge of the cap.

Make a row of stitching 2cm in from the edge of the cap. Make a second row 6mm away from the edge, forming a casing. Snip the fabric and thread a narrow tape through the casing with a bodkin (diagram 17e). Draw up the tape so that the cap fits the head loosely.

Stitch the mob cap to the head along the line of the casing covering the threads and raw edges at the back of the head, bringing it well down at the back of the head to cover the neck join.

Dress

Cut one dress bodice in half lengthways. These pieces will be the bodice back with a back opening. Stitch the front and back together at the shoulder seams (diagram 17f).

Cut a cross-cut strip of fabric 16cm × 4cm to bind the neck edge. Place one edge right sides together to the neck curve. Stitch taking a 6mm seam. Turn the binding to the inside. Fold under 6mm and hem the folded edge down on to the stitching line (diagram 18a).

Run a gathering thread along the curved head of the sleeve. Draw up the sleeve to fit the armhole and stitch right sides together (diagram 18b).

Stitch a narrow hem at the sleeve edge. Stretch an 8cm length of narrow elastic across the side of the sleeve 2cm from the hem. Stitch the stretched elastic to the sleeve using a zigzag stitch.

Join the sleeve and side seams.

Cut two strips of fabric 8cm long and 2cm wide. Stitch these, right sides together, to the back edges of the dress and turn to the inside to neaten. Stitch narrow velcro in place to fasten the bodice.

Stitch the short sides of the skirt piece together leaving the seam open for 4cm at one end. Run a gathering thread along this edge and ease it up to fit the bodice. Stitch the skirt to the bodice with the open end at the centre back. Neaten the dress hem with narrow lace.

Apron

Neaten the short sides of the apron skirt. Run a gathering thread along one long side and ease this up to fit the waistband strip, leaving a 6mm turning on the band at each side. Stitch. Neaten the sides of the band by folding the edges right sides together and stitching across the ends (diagram 18c). Turn the band right side out. Turn the raw edge under and hem to the stitching line. Stitch

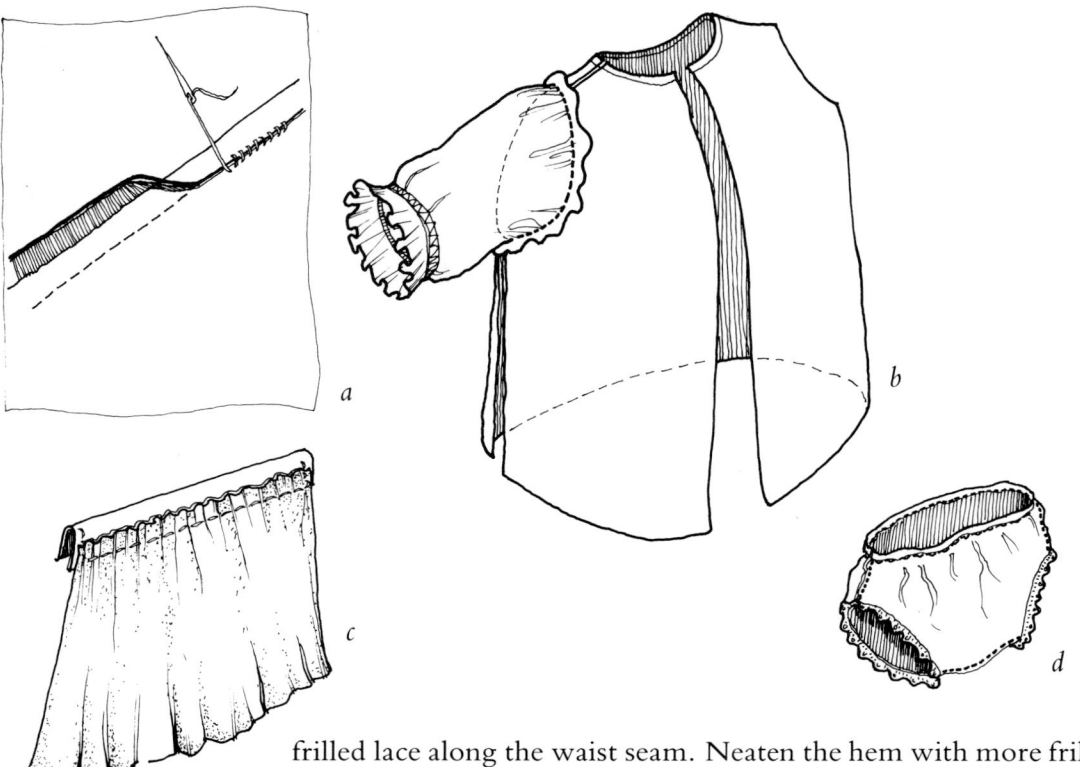

Diagram 18

frilled lace along the waist seam. Neaten the hem with more frilled lace.

Fold the straps in half down the length, right side out. Neaten the raw edges with frilled lace. Put the apron on the doll to find the position for the shoulder straps and stitch in place. Stitch ribbon ties to the back waist of the apron.

Pants

Join the short seam. Neaten the curved leg edges with lace. Fold in half right sides together and stitch the side seams (diagram 18d). Turn down 6mm at the top and stitch forming a casing. Thread through narrow elastic and draw up to fit the doll's waist.

32

4 Noah's Ark

Like a rocking horse or a toy fort, Noah's Ark is the type of toy which gives a permanence to childhood and is often handed down from parents to children. Toys like these are expensive to buy so this Ark made from fabric is an excellent substitute. It is sturdy and durable and will make a lovely present for a small child, or a general present for a young family.

Making this Noah's Ark could also be a family project during school holidays, since it is not at all difficult to make. The boat and roof are made from heavy ribbed corduroy while the animals and Mr and Mrs Noah are made from felt. They are cut as simple flat shapes with a little padding added.

Diagram 19

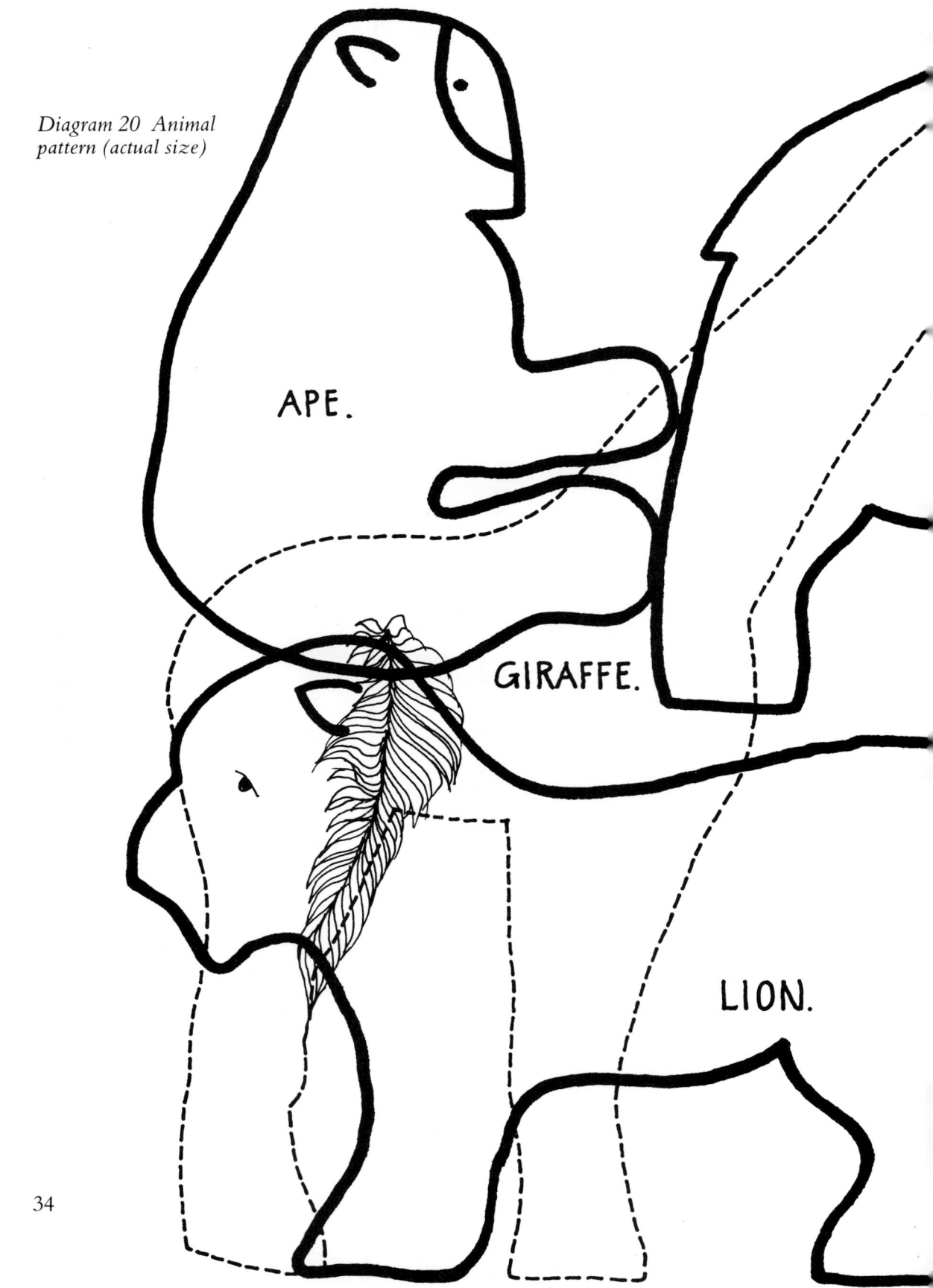

Diagram 20 Animal pattern (actual size)

APE.

GIRAFFE.

LION.

34

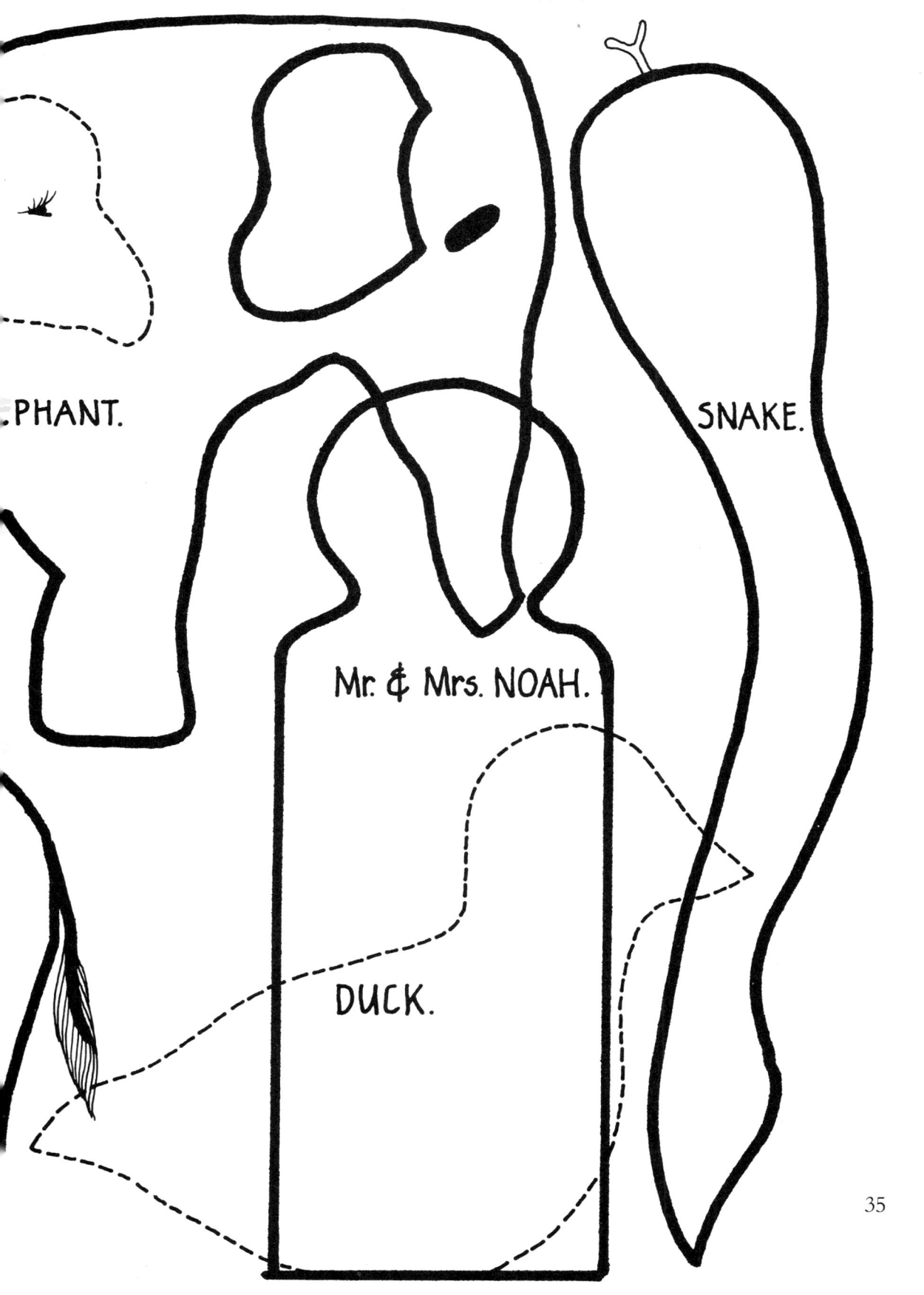

PHANT.

SNAKE.

Mr. & Mrs. NOAH.

DUCK.

35

Making the ark and animals

Cut out the pattern for the boat sides, bases, and roof of the ark in stiff paper, following these measurements. Trace the animals and Noah from the pattern shapes following the solid lines (diagram 20). Follow the broken line for the giraffe and duck.

Materials required

ARK
1.20m heavy ribbed corduroy 90cm wide
30cm beige-coloured cotton 90cm wide
200g polyester filling
Glue
Firm iron-on vilene interfacing
Stiff card
23cm square brown felt

Cutting out

1cm turnings are allowed on all the patterns. Cut out in corduroy – two bases, four roofs and four boat sides (diagram 21), following the cutting layout so that the rib of the corduroy lies in the direction shown. Cut out in cotton, one strip 21cm × 66cm for the house sides, and one house base. Cut two roofs and two boat sides in firm interfacing.

Diagram 21 Ark pattern

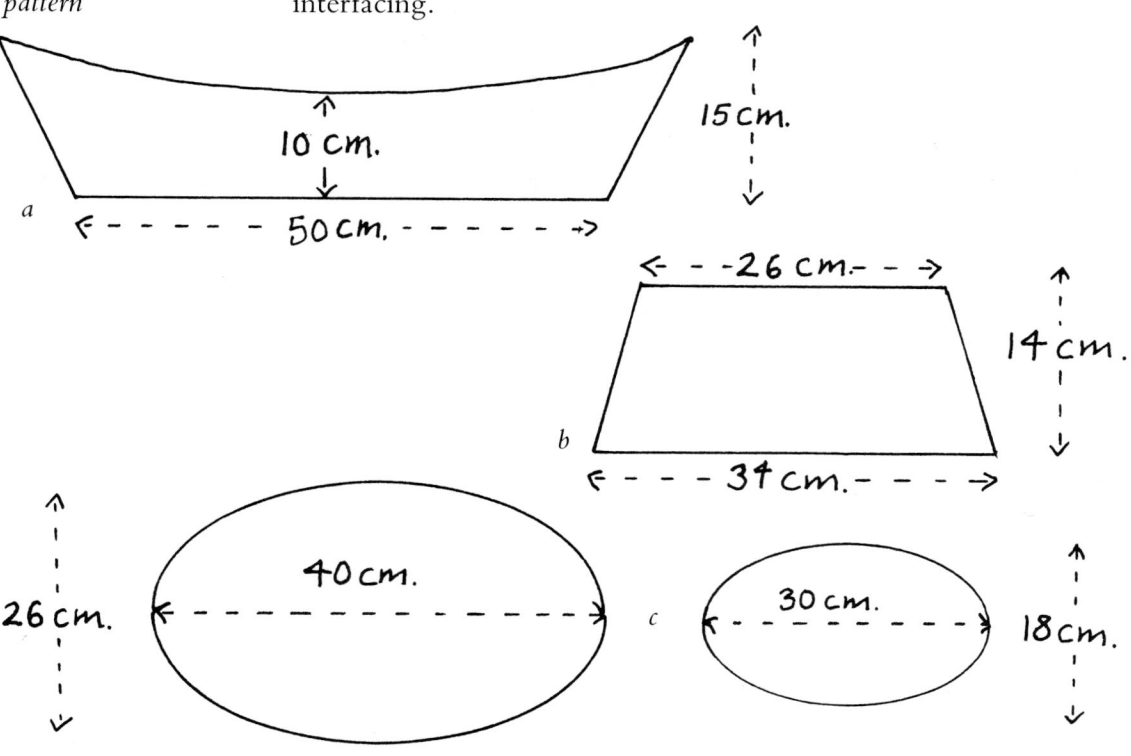

36

SEWING INSTRUCTIONS

Boat

Fuse the iron-on interfacing to the wrong side of two boat sides and two roof pieces.

Stitch the boat sides together, in pairs, along the short edge taking a 1cm seam (diagram 22).

Open out the interfaced sides into an oval shape, insert one base piece and, with right sides together, stitch the base to the sides – easing to fit.

Turn the boat right side out. Place the second boat side over the outside of the boat with right sides together. Stitch round the top edge. Turn this boat side to the inside. Edge stitch round the top edge of the boat.

Cut a piece of stiff card slightly smaller than the boat base pattern piece. Lay it on the wrong side of the second corduroy base piece. Spread glue round the edges of the card and fold in the turnings to cover the card edges. Spread the glue over the centre of the card and insert the covered base into the boat, fabric side uppermost. Press well down with the base concealing the raw edges of the inner boat sides.

House

Join the short sides of the cotton strip to form a circle. Insert the house base piece and stitch to one end, right sides together. Turn right side out. Cut a piece of card slightly smaller than the house base pattern and insert into the base. Stuff firmly to within 2.5cm of the top. Turn the raw edges over the stuffing and lace the edges of the opening together with thread (diagram 23).

From the remaining cotton fabric cut a strip large enough to cover the opening. Turn in the raw edges of this strip and hem in place over the opening. Spread glue over the house base and glue to the boat base. Allow to dry. Reinforce with several stitches at the corners of the base.

Roof

Stitch the roof pieces together in pairs, round the outside edges, leaving an opening of about 8cm. Turn inside-out through the opening (diagram 24).

Oversew the opening together. Stitch the two roof sections together along the top 6mm away from the edge forming a ridge. Catch stitch the roof to the house at each side.

Cut a curved door from a rectangle of brown felt 13cm × 6cm and windows 4cm square. Glue these in place on the house and add cross strips of beige felt to the windows.

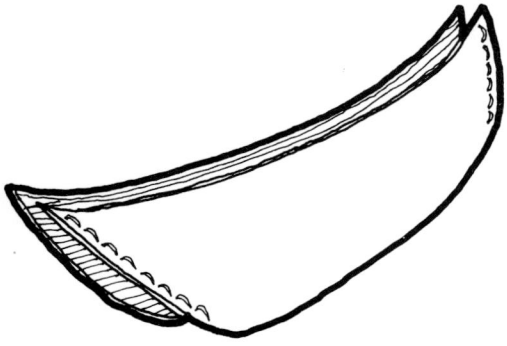

stitch boat sides together
with right sides facing in...

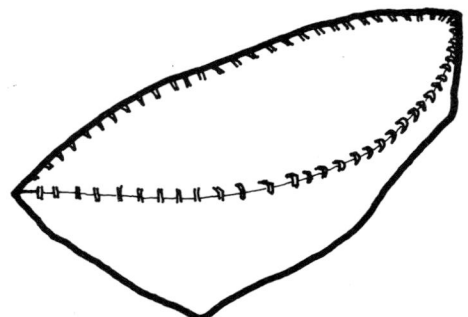

stitch first base to interfaced
sides to form boat shape.

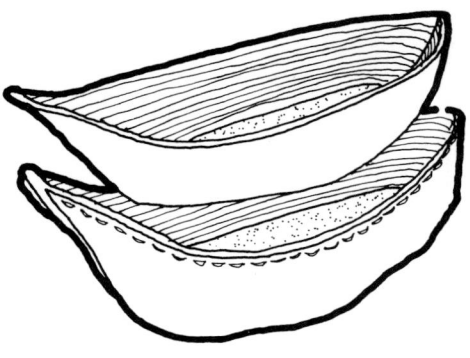

place second boat sides over
hull and stitch along top edge...

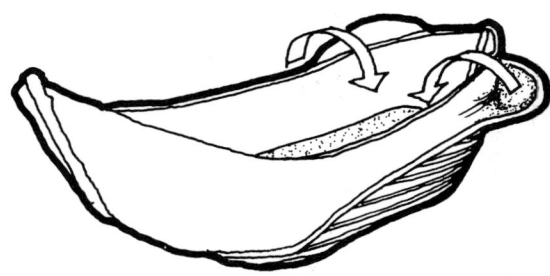

turn outside into the inside
of hull to expose corduroy...

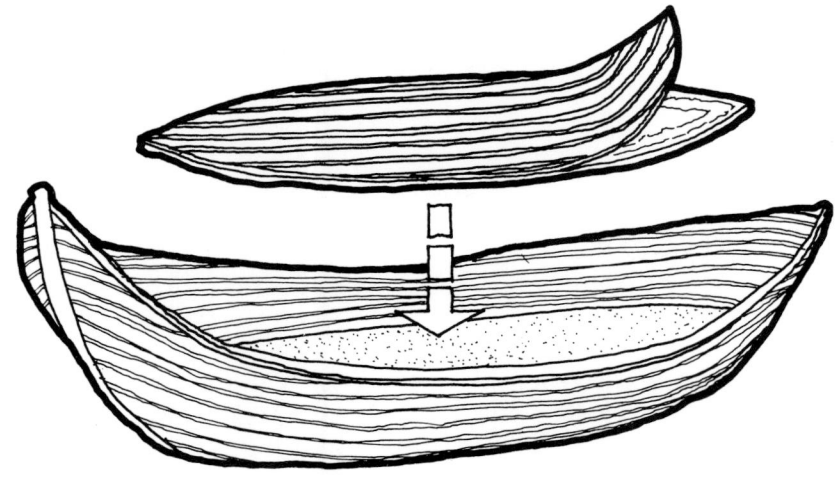

Diagram 22
Construction of the boat

glue fabric to cardboard then
glue securely into base of boat.

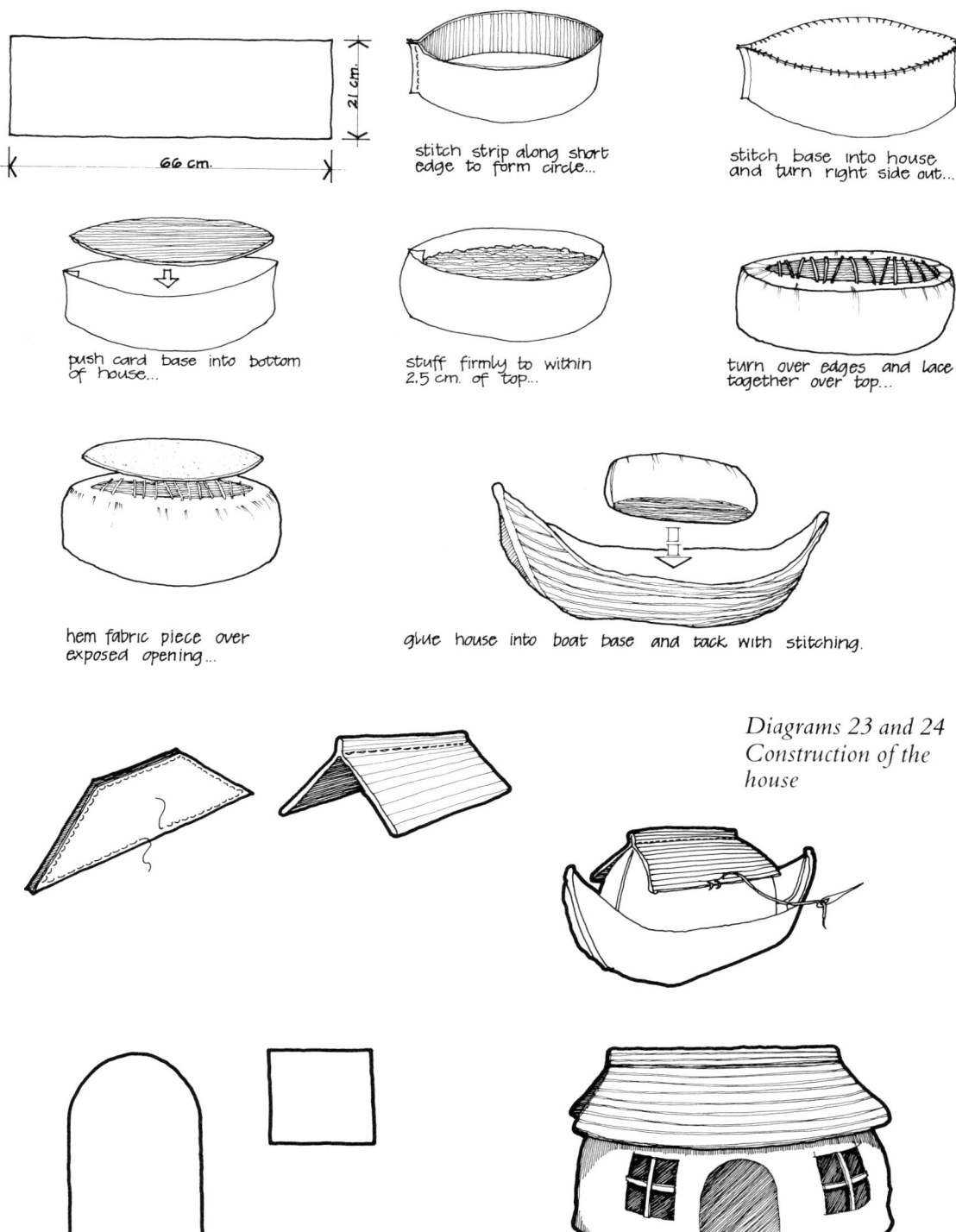

66 cm.

21 cm.

stitch strip along short
edge to form circle...

stitch base into house
and turn right side out...

push card base into bottom
of house...

stuff firmly to within
2.5 cm. of top...

turn over edges and lace
together over top...

hem fabric piece over
exposed opening...

glue house into boat base and tack with stitching.

*Diagrams 23 and 24
Construction of the
house*

Materials required

ANIMALS AND MR AND MRS NOAH

Elephants	30cm square grey felt
Giraffes	2 × 30cm square orange felt
	Scraps of brown felt
Apes	23cm square brown felt
	Scrap of beige felt
Lions	30cm square yellow felt
	Scrap fur fabric or yellow felt
Snakes	23cm square green felt
	Scrap of orange felt
	2 × 20 cm lengths florist wire
Ducks	23cm square cream felt
Mr and Mrs Noah	20cm square beige felt
	23cm square fawn felt
	Scraps green felt
	23cm square blue felt

Construction

SEWING INSTRUCTIONS

Elephant

Cut two body shapes and four ear shapes. Stitch the ear shapes together round the curved edges 5mm from the outer edge. Stitch the ears to the body along the straight edge as shown. Join the two body pieces, leaving an opening about 5cm long in the back. Leave open at the feet. Insert enough stuffing through the openings to form a well-padded animal (use a cocktail stick to push the stuffing into the legs). Stitch across the openings. Draw the eye in black felt pen.

Giraffe

Cut out two body shapes. Stitch together and stuff as above. Cut a strip of felt 3cm × 5cm. Fringe one end and stitch in place for a tail. Cut irregular-shaped spots in brown felt and glue on the neck and back of the giraffe. Draw the eye in felt pen where shown.

Ape

Cut two body shapes. Stitch and stuff. Cut two ear shapes. Stitch to the head where shown. Cut the front face in cream felt. Glue or stitch in place. Draw the eye in felt pen where shown.

Lion

Cut two body shapes. Stitch and stuff. Cut a fringe of felt 2.5cm deep, long enough to encircle the head (or use a scrap of long-pile fur). Stitch or glue the mane to the head on the dotted line. Add a tail, as for the giraffe, and small ears in front of the mane from a scrap of felt. Draw in the eyes.

Snake

Cut two body shapes. Stitch round the outer edges leaving an opening. Turn the ends of the wire into a loop. Insert the wire into the body of the snake. Add a little stuffing. Stitch the opening. Cut a forked tongue in orange felt and stitch to the underside of the front of the head. Bend the snake into a coil. Mark spots on the back of the head in red felt pen.

Duck

Cut two body shapes. Stitch and stuff. Cut a beak and wings in orange felt and glue in place.

Noah

Cut two body shapes. Stitch round the outer edges leaving open at the base. Stuff firmly. Stand the body on a piece of thick card and draw round the base. Cut out this oval shape and insert into the base. Cut a second oval shape slightly larger in felt and stitch in place to form the base of the figure.

Cut a semi-circle of fawn felt with the diameter 25cm (see diagram 25). Wrap round the body to form a cloak. Cut the point

Diagram 25

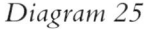

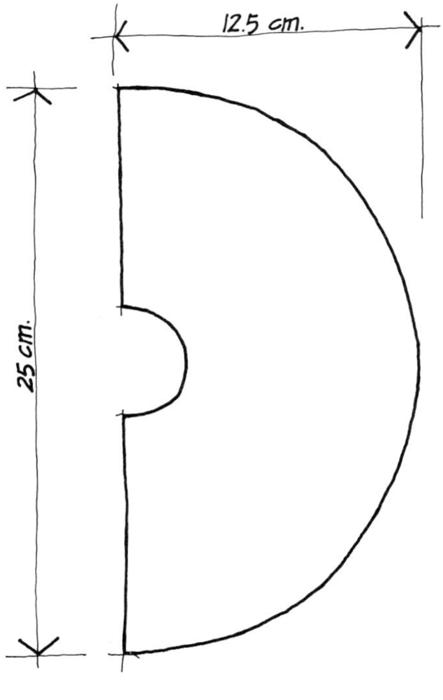

12.5 cm.

25 cm.

Cloak

mr. & mrs. noah.

41

into a curve to fit the neck of the figure. Cut a semi–circle, diameter 16cm, in green felt. Wrap round the body to form a shawl.

Cut a strip of fawn felt 10cm × 4cm. Drape this over the head. Stitch in place, easing the fabric into folds. Tie a narrow strip of green felt around the top of the head.

Mrs Noah

Make the body as for Noah. Cut a semi–circle of blue felt, diameter 25cm. Overlap it round the body to form a cloak. Stitch in place. Cover the head as for Noah, tying a strip of blue felt around the top of the head.

Gifts

5 Novelty Aprons for Children

Diagram 26 Rabbit apron

Toddlers and young children will love these unusual aprons which are also great fun to make. The apron bib is made to look like a teddy bear's or rabbit's face and the skirt of the apron looks like the dress that the teddy or rabbit is wearing (diagrams 26 and 27).

Diagram 27 Teddy bear apron

Both aprons are made from this simple pattern. The pattern shape for the apron bib is attached with the widest part at the top to make the teddy bear's head, and it is reversed and used with the narrowest part at the top to make the rabbit's head. The length of the apron skirt can be adjusted according to any size of child. The length suggested here is for a child of two to four years.

Making the apron pattern

Using stiff plain paper, draw out the pattern shapes following the diagrams and the measurements given. 6mm seam turnings are allowed on the pattern.

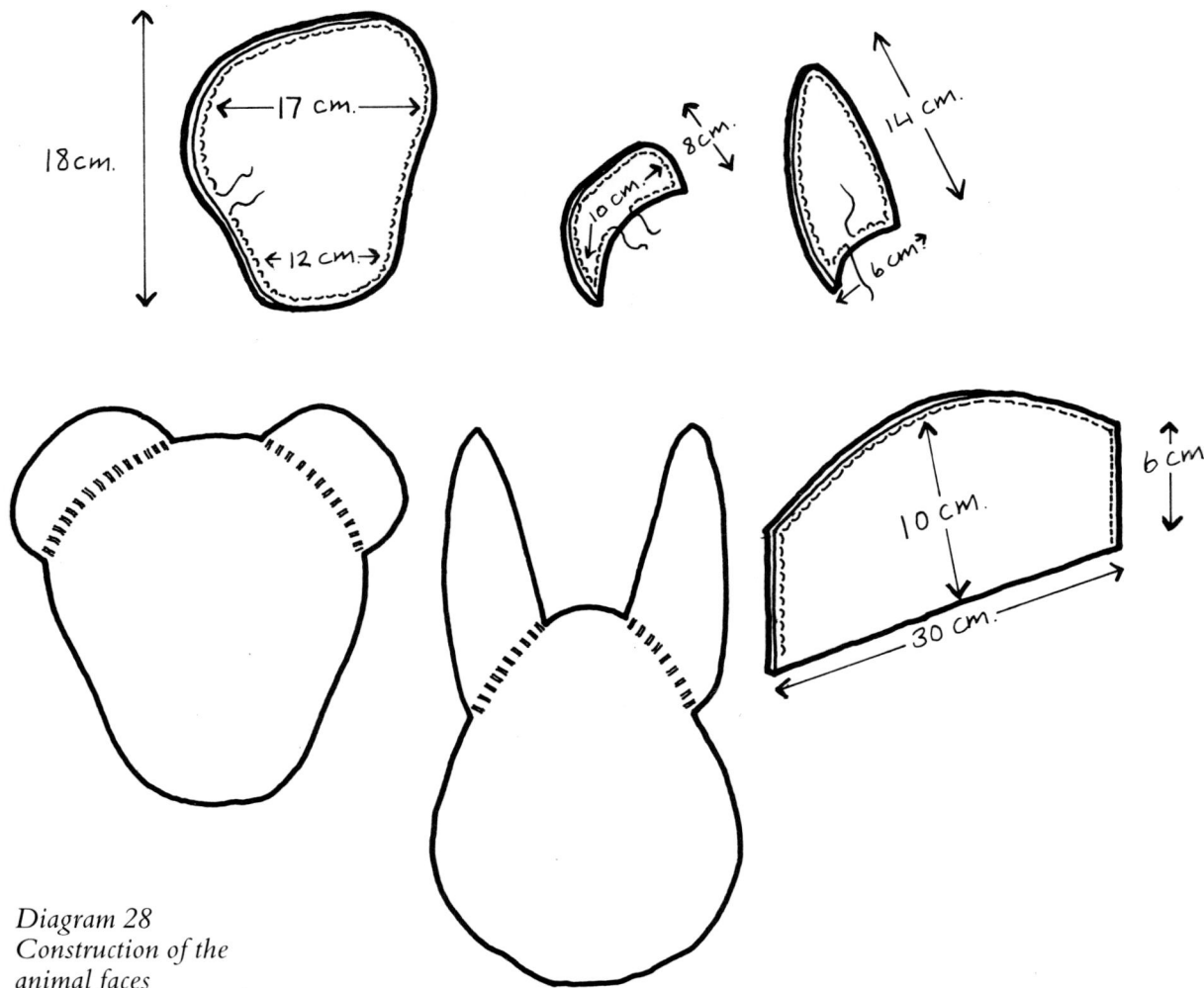

Diagram 28
Construction of the
animal faces

40cm yellow cotton (teddy bear) or white cotton (rabbit), 90cm wide
40cm spotted or gingham fabric 90cm wide
Scrap black fabric
1m lace trimming 1.5cm wide
60cm tape
Black embroidery thread

In yellow or white fabric cut out two heads, four ears and four feet, following the cutting layout given. Cut two strips across the width of the fabric for the arms, 10cm × 60cm.

In spotted or gingham fabric cut two yokes and a strip of fabric for the apron skirt 60cm wide × 30cm long.

SEWING INSTRUCTIONS
With the right sides together, stitch the head pieces round the outside taking a 6mm seam, leaving an opening of approximately 5cm. Turn right side out through the opening and stitch the opening together. Press.

Stitch the ears, in pairs, round the outside edges, leaving an opening. Turn right side out. Slip stitch the opening together. Press.

Teddy bear apron
Oversew the ears to the widest part of the head at the sides.

Rabbit apron
Oversew the straight edge of the ears to the narrowest part of the head at the sides.

With the right sides to the inside, stitch the yoke pieces together along the curved edge and down the short sides. Turn the yoke right side out. Press.

Neaten the two short sides of the apron skirt with a narrow hem. Run a gathering thread along one long side, 6mm away from the edge.

Draw up the skirt to fit the yoke. With right sides together place one raw edge of the yoke to the gathered edge of the skirt. Tack and stitch (diagram 29).

Turn under 6mm on the other yoke edge and bring it down to the stitching line enclosing the turnings. Hem in place.

Neaten the skirt hem with lace. Stitch the feet in pairs in the same way as the ears. Oversew to the hem of the skirt so that they peep out below the lace.

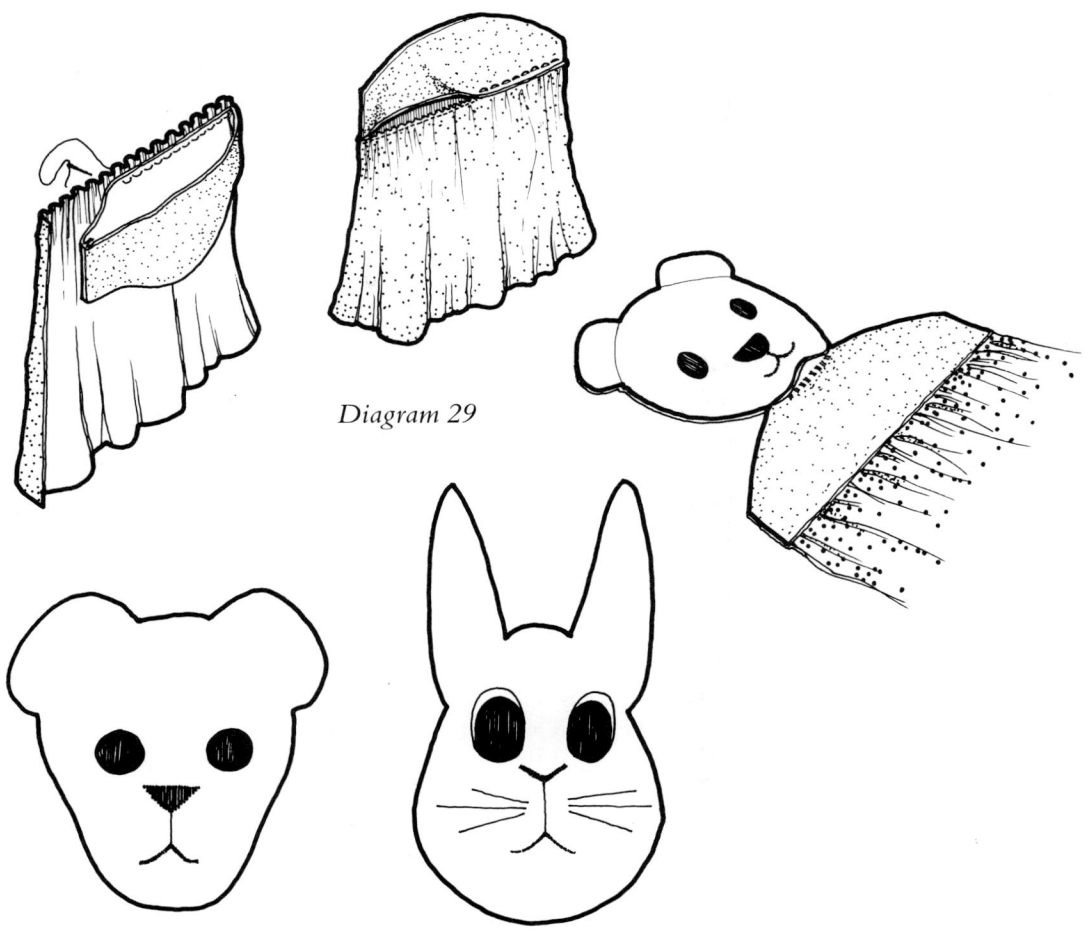

Diagram 29

Diagram 30 Animal features

Oversew the back of the head to the centre of the yoke, allowing the head to overlap the yoke by 2cm. Stitch lace trimming to form an outline of a collar on the yoke.

Fold the strips of fabric in half along the length. Stitch down the raw edges and along one end, taking a 6mm seam. Turn them inside out and press.

Stitch these strips to the sides of the yoke to form the arms and to tie the apron round the waist. Stitch a tape on each ear to tie the apron round the neck.

A small pocket can be added to the apron skirt. To do this, cut a piece of fabric approximately 8cm square. Neaten one edge with lace for the top of the pocket. Turn in the raw edges on the other three sides and stitch in place on the skirt.

Stitch two circles of black fabric halfway down the head for the eyes, and embroider the nose detail as shown in diagram 30.

6 Quilted Table Mats

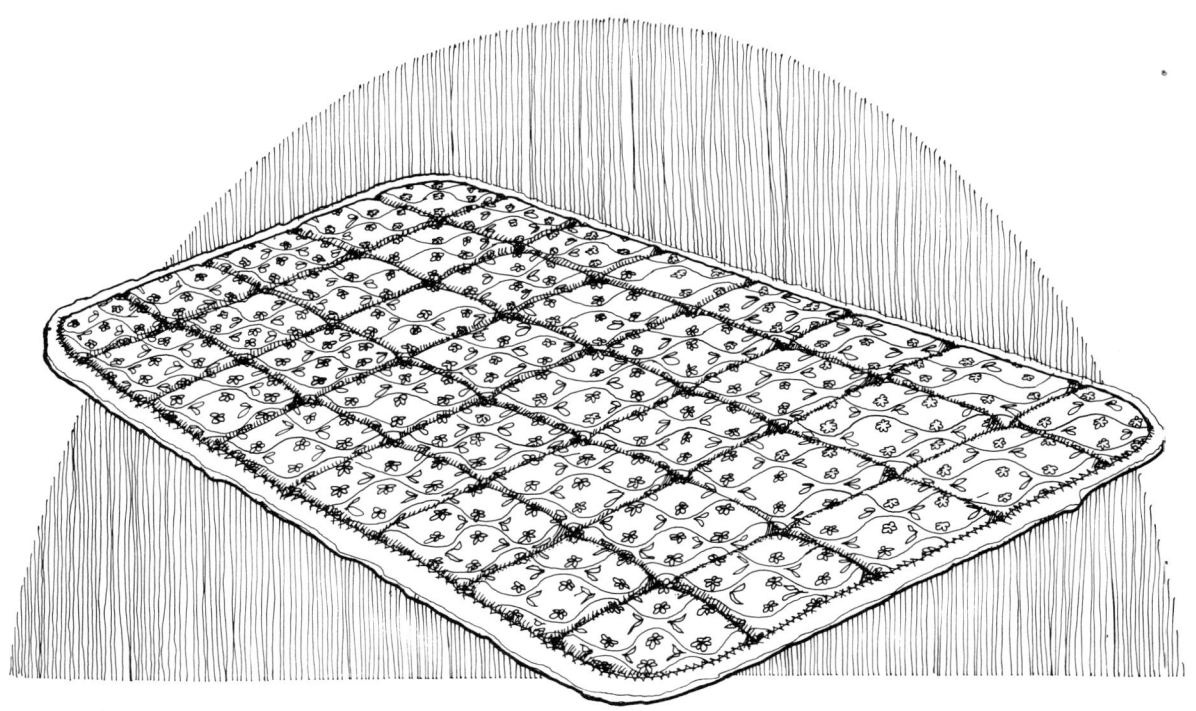

Diagram 31

These mats are ideal for the informal meals that most of us eat in the kitchen (diagram 31). They are made from two layers of fabric with a layer of washable polyester wadding between, which means they are reasonably heat proof and are reversible. You can also incorporate two fabrics in one mat – a plain fabric on one side and a patterned fabric on the other. You could, for example, use the fabric of your kitchen curtains combined with a fabric in the colour of your pottery or kitchen colour scheme.

The mats are edged with a folded plain ribbon, toning with both sides of the mats and stitched with a zigzag or feather stitch. They measure 45cm × 30cm.

Materials required

TO MAKE SIX MATS

1m plain fabric 90cm wide
1m patterned fabric 90cm wide
1m polyester wadding 90cm wide and 6mm thick
9m double-edged satin ribbon 1.5cm wide

Construction

SEWING INSTRUCTIONS

Cut each of the fabrics into six pieces 45cm × 30cm. Lay one fabric right side down on the table. Place the wadding on top and the second fabric right side uppermost having all the edges even. Tack through all three layers, round the outside edges and diagonally across from corner to corner, keeping the work flat on the table as you tack (diagram 32).

QUILTING THE TABLEMATS

Most machines incorporate a quilting attachment and this saves a great deal of drawing and measuring lines. The attachment is a very simple one and often lies in the sewing box without recognition. It consists basically of a metal rod with a bend at one end (diagram 33). How it is attached to the machine varies according to the type of machine but it is very simple to use and the instructions will be in your sewing machine manual. The rod is fixed to the presser foot and the distance from the bent end of the rod to the machine needle determines the width between the lines of stitching. Set the attachment so that this distance is 5cm. (If your machine does not have this attachment, rule faint pencil lines both ways across the mat, 5cm apart). If you are using a quilting attachment rule one line each way 5cm from the edge, as a guide for the first line of stitching.

Reduce the pressure of the machine foot and set the length to the longest stitch. Stitch down the first marked line. Place the edge of the quilting foot on this line and stitch a second parallel line holding the work taut as you stitch and always stitching in the same direction. Complete the stitching lines in this direction and then stitch across them at right angles to form 5cm squares.

FINISHING THE EDGES

Trim the outside edges evenly and round off the corners of the mats into a curve. (This will avoid having to mitre the corners.) Press the ribbon in half along its length. Tack the folded ribbon over the edges of the mat. Stitch using a feather stitch or a wide zigzag stitch.

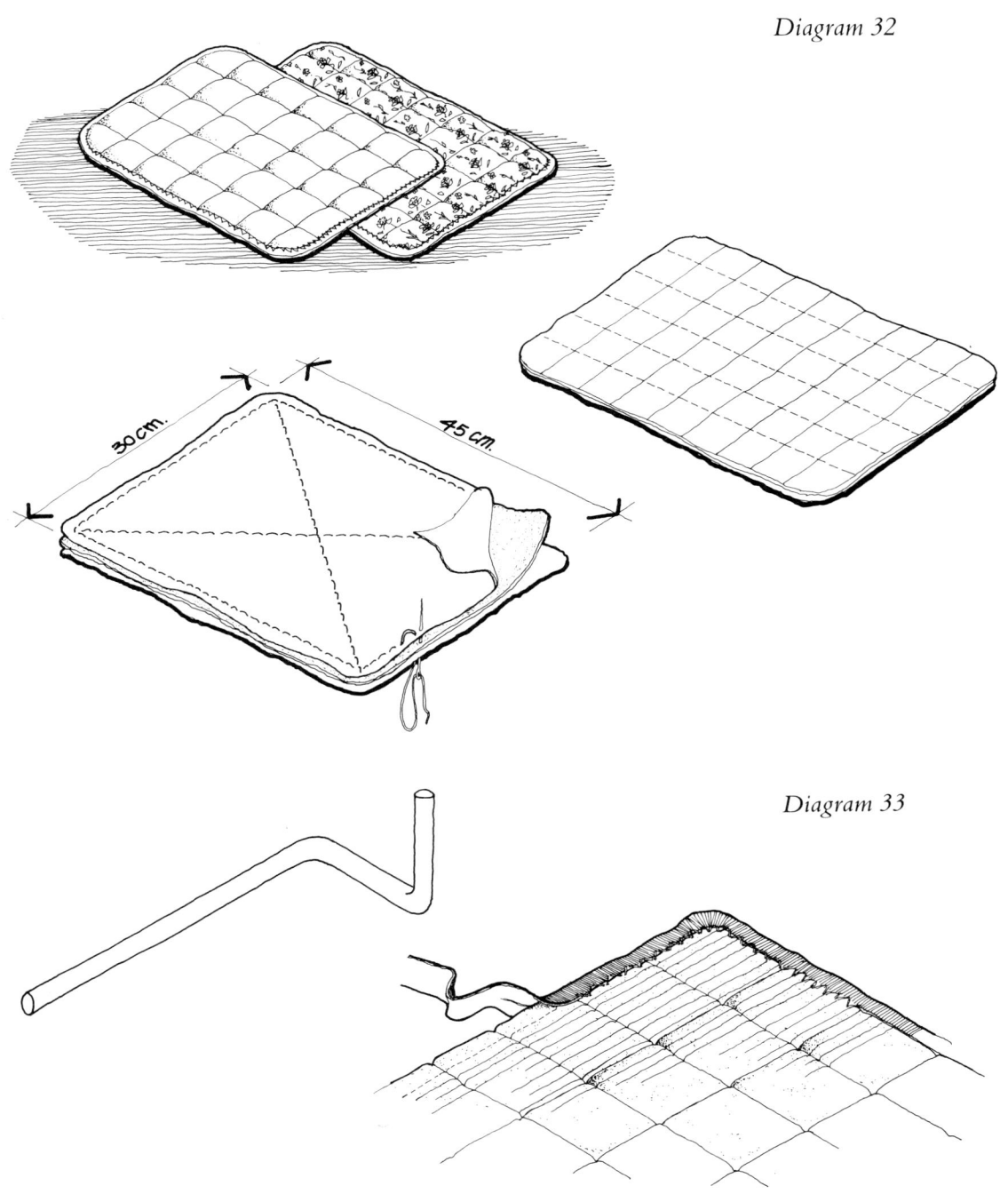

Diagram 32

30 cm.

45 cm.

Diagram 33

7 Made-to-Measure Tablecloths

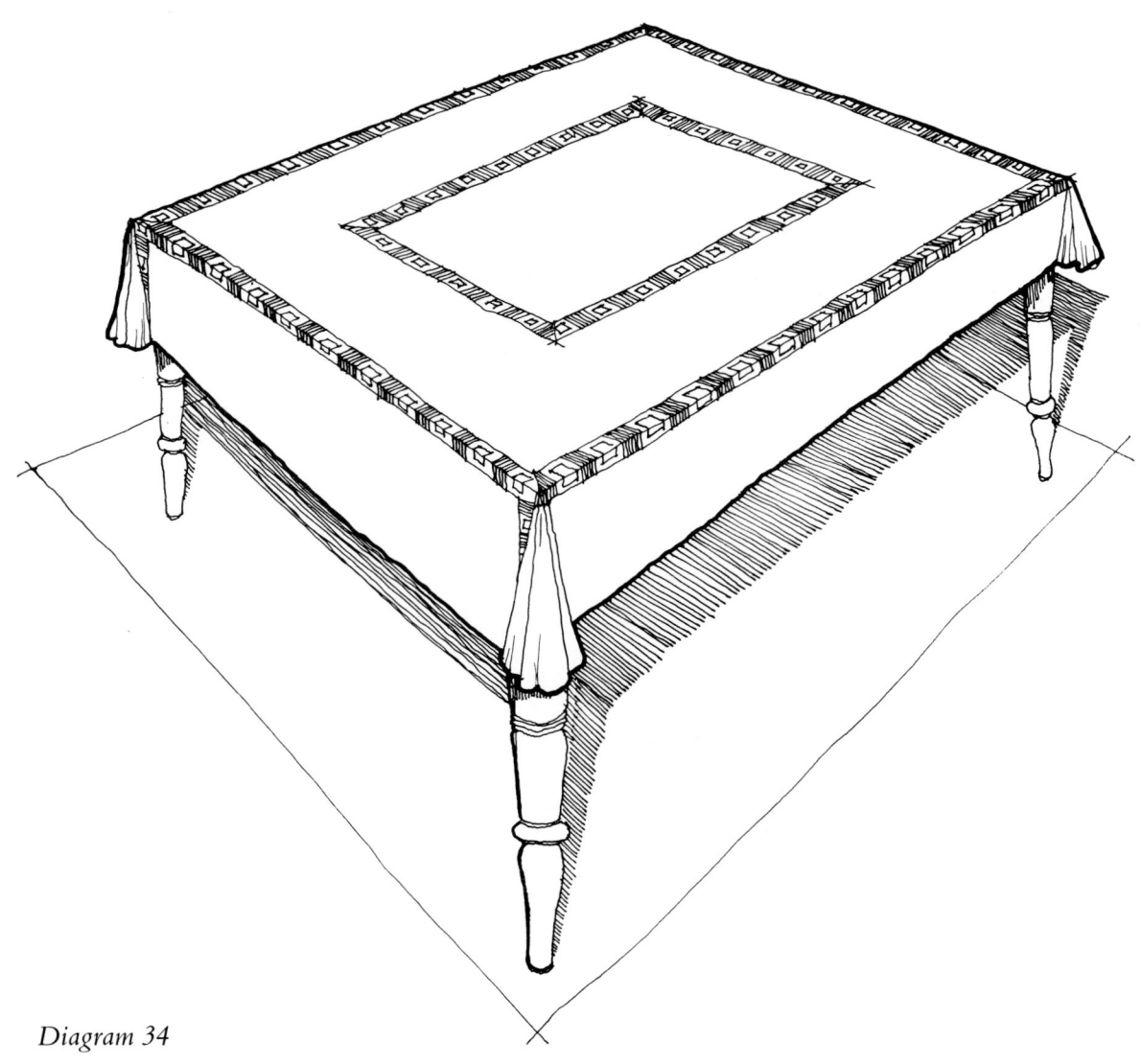

Diagram 34

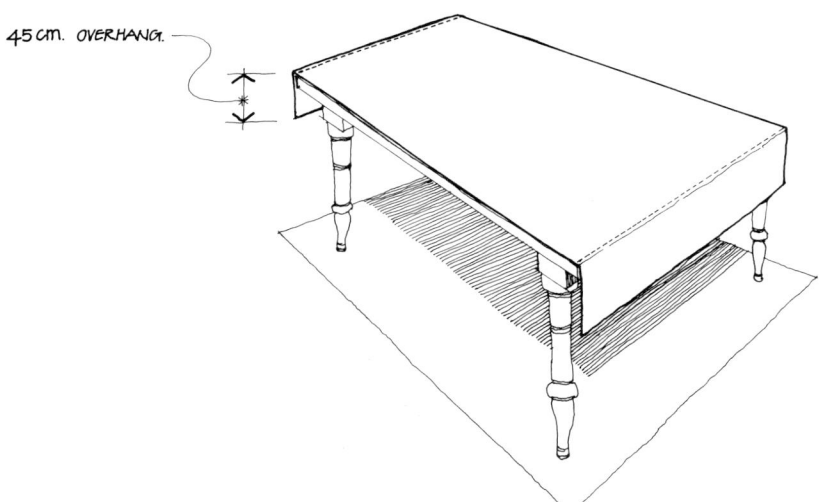

45 CM. OVERHANG.

If you have ever tried to find an extra special cloth for an important occasion, or a cloth to match a particular dinner service, or to fit an extra large table, you will know how difficult it can be to find exactly what you need. This pattern can be adjusted to fit any table. The table edges are outlined with a wide embroidered ribbon which looks extremely smart and also conceals the seams in the fabric to enable you to make a very large cloth (diagram 34). The matching table napkins are trimmed with a narrower version of the same embroidered ribbon.

Choose a heavy polyester/cotton fabric for the cloth in a strong colour. This creates a relaxed and less formal atmosphere than white or cream and is a perfect foil for modern pottery, glass and flowers. A dark brown cloth trimmed with beige and white ribbon used with terra cotta pottery is an effective colour scheme, as is a navy cloth with a white trim and white and yellow pottery.

A tablecloth, tailored to size and matching the bride's own china would make a delightful wedding gift.

TABLECLOTH

Materials required

Fabric: twice the length of your table, plus 90cm. The width of the fabric you will need will depend on the width of your table. For a table 102cm wide, use fabric 115cm wide. For a table 76cm wide, fabric 90cm wide can be used. Choose a plain heavy polyester/cotton fabric with a pronounced weave. The fabric should be the same on both sides, i.e. have no definite right or wrong side.

Ribbon: estimated when you have stitched the sections of the tablecloth together to fit your table. You will need twice the length of the finished cloth plus twice the width. The ribbon should be

2.5cm wide, to cover the seam lines and to stitch across the width of the cloth at the table edge; and twice the length of the table plus twice the width, less 80cm, of the same ribbon in a narrower width to complete the design as in the diagram.

Construction

SEWING INSTRUCTIONS

Cut the length of fabric in half across the width. Place one of these pieces over the table, allowing it to hang down evenly at each end by 45cm. Slide the fabric across the table so that the selvedge is exactly at the edge at one side. Cut the surplus fabric from the other edge so that the cloth fits the table width exactly. (You will find it easier to draw a pencil line along the table edge before cutting.)

Draw a pencil line across the width of the table edge at each end. This marks the position for the ribbon trim (diagram 35). Fold the second length of fabric in half lengthwise and pin the selvedges together. Rule a pencil line 46cm from the selvedges and cut away the surplus fabric on this line (diagram 35). Place the cut edges of these strips to the long sides of the tablecloth. Stitch them together taking a 1cm seam. Press the seams open.

Attaching the ribbon

Lay the cloth on the table, *seam turnings uppermost*. Place the 2.5cm wide ribbon over the seam turnings, pin and tack. Pin and tack the ribbon to the inside of the placement lines across the width, extending these lines to the edge of the cloth.

Rule a pencil line 13cm from these lines of ribbon (which outline the table edge) forming a rectangle. Starting at one corner, pin and tack the narrower ribbon on these lines. Turn the ribbon at right angles to form a mitre at the corners and conceal the ends of the ribbon, where they meet, in a mitre.

Stitching the ribbon

This is an opportunity to make the most of the embroidery stitches on your sewing machine. (If you just have a basic machine the ribbon can be attached with a straight stitch or a wide zigzag.) The commonest stitch found on all but the most basic machines is the feather stitch and this is an excellent stitch to attach the ribbon. Choose a thread which is a good match for the ribbon edge, and stitch with the presser foot centred along this edge so that half of the feather stitching is on the ribbon and half on the fabric. This gives the effect of the ribbon being woven into the fabric rather than placed on the top. If you have a wide choice of embroidery stitches on your machine you can experiment to see which gives the best effect.

Diagram 35

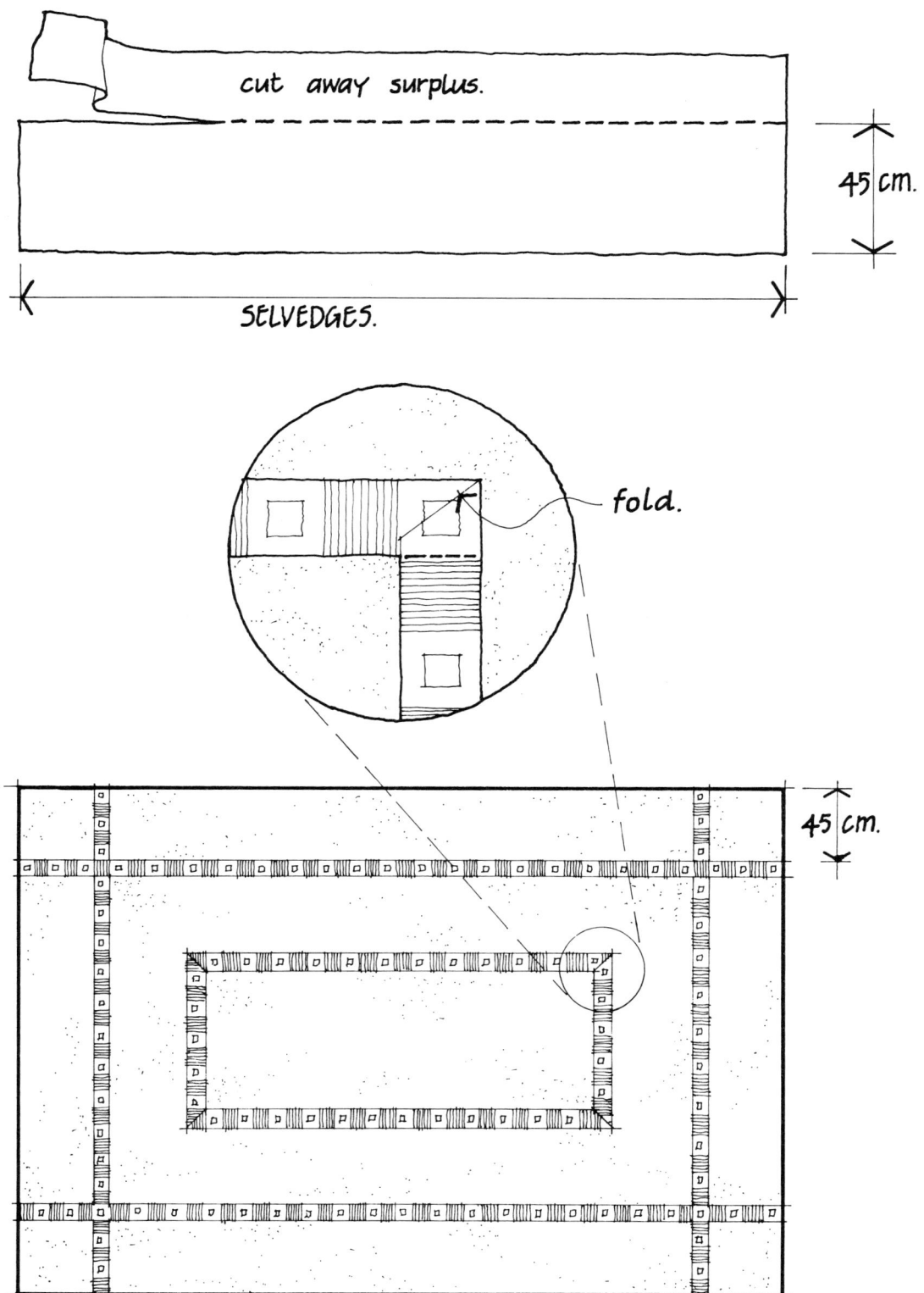

cut away surplus.

45 cm.

SELVEDGES.

fold.

45 cm.

Finishing the edges of the cloth

The two long sides are selvedges and need no further finishing. Turn under a narrow hem (about 6mm) on the raw edges of the short sides of the cloth and stitch using a straight or feather stitch.

Materials required

NAPKINS
80cm of fabric 115cm wide
9m of ribbon 1cm wide (Makes 6, 38cm square)

Construction

Cut the napkins accurately on the straight thread of the fabric. Pencil a line 1.5cm from the edge on all four sides. Place one edge of the ribbon to the inside of this line and machine using a small stitch, on the ribbon edge. Fold the ribbon at right angles at the corners, forming a mitre.

Stitch the other ribbon edge with a feather stitch as for the tablecloth. Press.

Fray out the raw edges of the napkins as far as the ribbon.

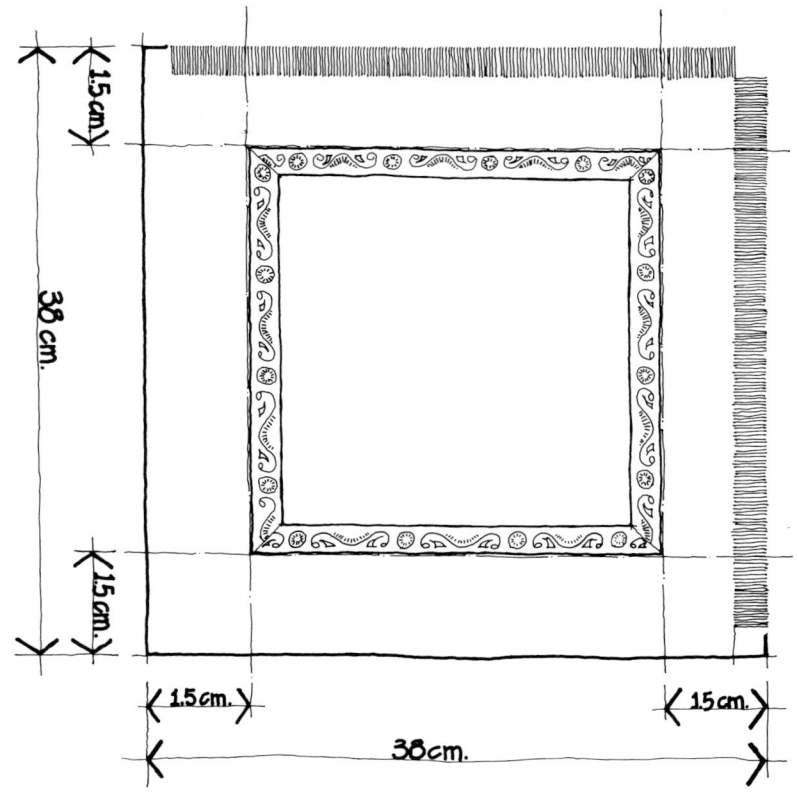

Diagram 36 Napkin

Decorations

8 Christmas Crackers

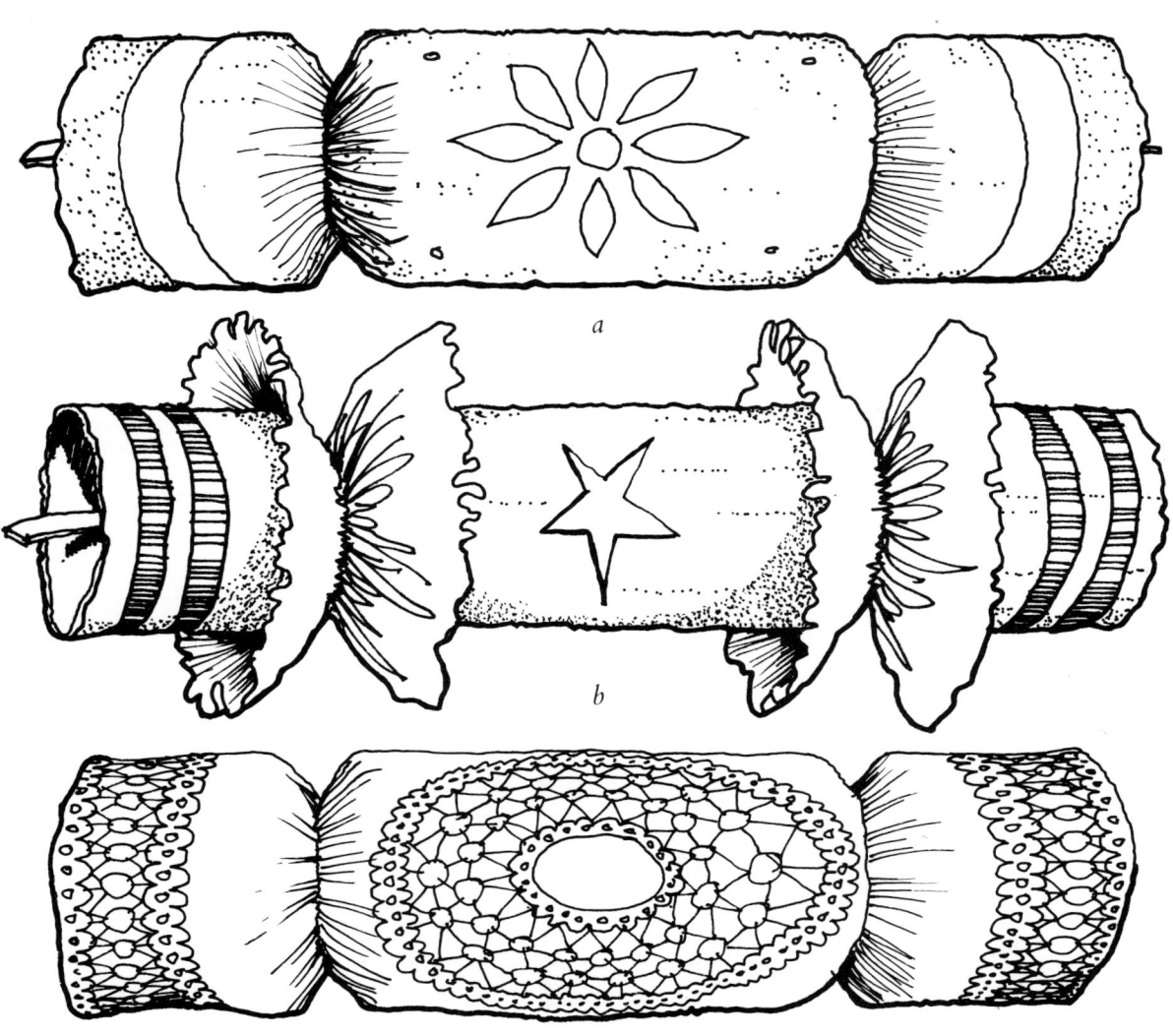

a

b

c

Diagram 37

Christmas crackers are often a disappointment. They look festive and exciting on the Christmas dinner table, but when they are pulled the contents of the cracker rarely live up to their promising appearance.

So why not make your own? This way you can use your original ideas in their decoration, and you can choose the fillings for the crackers yourself.

Crackers are easy to make and the simplest way to learn to make your own is to buy a kit. The kits include all the basic requirements – crepe paper, lining paper, formers (these are metal or cardboard tubes which shape the cracker), snaps, thin card, mottos, hats and an assortment of foil and scraps for decoration. They do not include gifts and for these you can use small toys, pencil sharpeners, rubbers, jewellery, miniature chocolate bars and chocolate liqueurs, jelly babies, thimbles, tightly rolled handkerchiefs, key rings or anything you like which is small enough.

Cracker kits are usually fairly basic and once you understand how to make up a cracker, you can then be very adventurous in their decoration and size. Substitutes are easily made for all the component parts, except the snaps, which you will have to buy. Names and addresses of stockists of Christmas cracker kits, and those who supply snaps, mottos and paper hats separately are listed at the end of the book.

Materials required

A sheet of crepe paper measuring 30cm × 17cm, the grain running lengthwise

Sheet of lining paper measuring 28cm × 15cm (use a very thin paper for this)

Piece of thin card 15cm × 9cm

Cracker snap

Paper hat (you can make a simple 'crown' of tissue paper or more elaborate hats in crepe paper)

Motto and a small gift

To shape the cracker you need a pair of formers. Make these from a stiff cardboard tube, diameter approximately 4cm. The stiff inner cardboard tube from a roll of kitchen foil or dress fabric will do. Make one former about 20cm long and the other about 15cm. You will also need some adhesive and a length of fine string.

ASSEMBLING THE CRACKER

Place the crepe paper flat on the table. Lay the lining paper on top. Place the snap lengthwise and lay the thin card centres across it.

Run a line of glue along the top edge of the papers.

Place the two formers in position, the smaller at the right hand side, so that the edges of the formers meet at the right hand edge of the piece of card. Roll up the cracker very tightly around the formers and hold in place to allow the glue to dry.

Ease out the smaller right hand former about 2.5cm. Wrap the string around the cracker over the gap between the two formers. Pull the string very tightly to draw in the paper. Push the right hand former against the other former to shape the end of the cracker. Remove the right hand former and the string.

Insert the hat, motto and gift into the other former. Draw out the former until the right hand edge is about 2.5cm from the left hand edge of the thin card. Check that the filling has slipped out of the former into the centre of the cracker. Wrap the string round the cracker as before and pull tightly. Shape the other end of the cracker. Remove the former and string.

If you wish to fill a cracker with an expensive gift or a heavy item, tie the cracker tightly with gold thread at each end to prevent the filling falling out.

DECORATING THE CRACKERS

The quickest way to finish off the crackers is simply to glue a band of coloured foil round the ends of the cracker and a cut-out scrap or a motif on top. You can create some very pretty crackers for a special occasion by decorating the crepe paper before you roll up the cracker, using gift-wrap ribbon, or a gold paper doily or by adding an extra layer of crepe paper at each end to form a ruff.

Some suggestions

Spread adhesive at each end of the crepe paper to a depth of 2.5cm. Sprinkle with gold or silver glitter. Glue a band of gold or silver gift ribbon about 1cm away from the edging of glitter. Make up the cracker in the usual way. Cut five petal shapes of ribbon, and glue them on top of the cracker to form a flower, adding a little glitter to the centre of the flower (diagram 37a).

Frilled crackers

These can look very exciting and are expensive to buy but easy to make.

Glue two bands of gift wrap ribbon about 1cm apart at each end of the crepe paper. Make up the cracker in the usual way. Cut a piece of crepe paper 10cm × 30cm, with the grain running widthwise. Fold in half down the length. Open it out and gather up the paper down this crease. Place the frill centred over the indent at one end of the cracker. Wrap a thread round the crease and pull the thread very tightly to form a ruff. Knot the thread and cut off the ends. Add a frill to the other end of the cracker, and glue a motif to the top of the cracker (diagram 37b).

Use a gold doily to trim the cracker making use of the pattern on the doily to suggest a design, for example, use the outer scalloped edge of the doily for the cracker ends and cut the centre of the doily for a motif for the top of the cracker (diagram 37c).

Form attractive tulip-shaped ends on the cracker by adding a double layer of shaped crepe paper at each end. Spread adhesive at each end of the crepe paper to a depth of 2.5cm. Sprinkle with gold

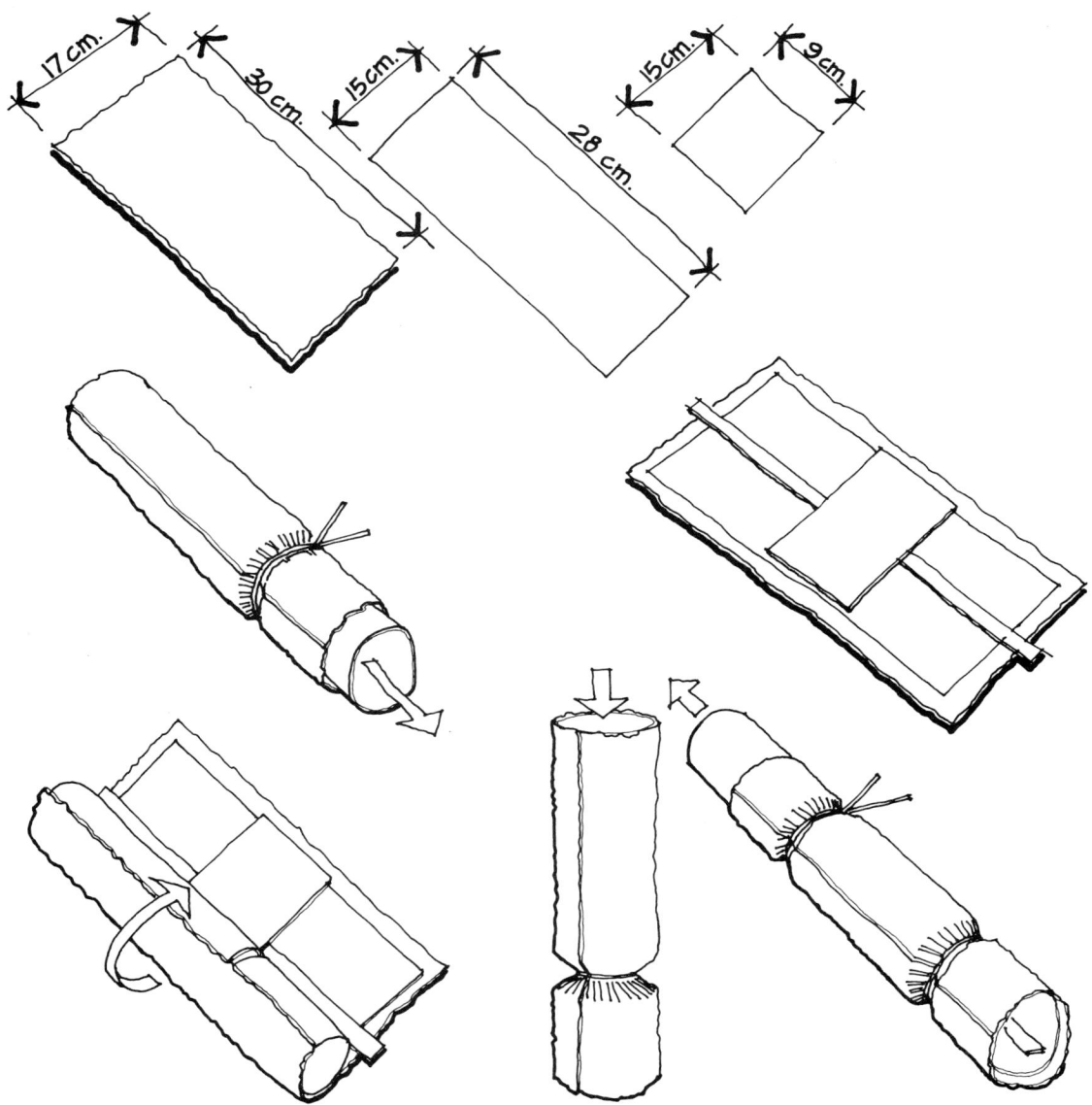

or silver glitter. Cut two pieces of crepe paper 11cm × 16cm with the grain running widthwise. Fold in half down the length. Cut the long side of each piece of paper into deep scallops. Unfold and tie the paper to the cracker end placing the fold over the indent of the cracker. Fold both edges of the paper towards the outside of the cracker, and using a pencil, roll back the scalloped edges so that they curl back revealing the glittered edges underneath.

Diagram 38 Making Christmas crackers

9 Fun with Fir Cones

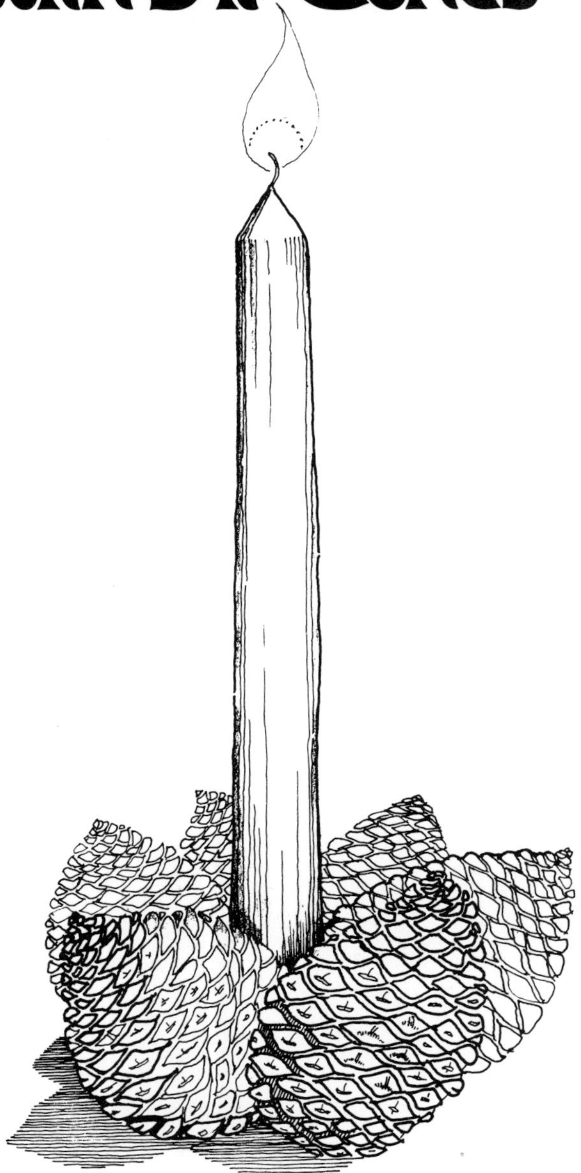

Diagram 39 Fir cone candlestick

Fir cones immediately evoke an image of Christmas. With their rough texture, sturdy shape and the faint scent of pine woods which lingers in even the driest cones, a cluster of fir cones is a pleasing decoration in itself.

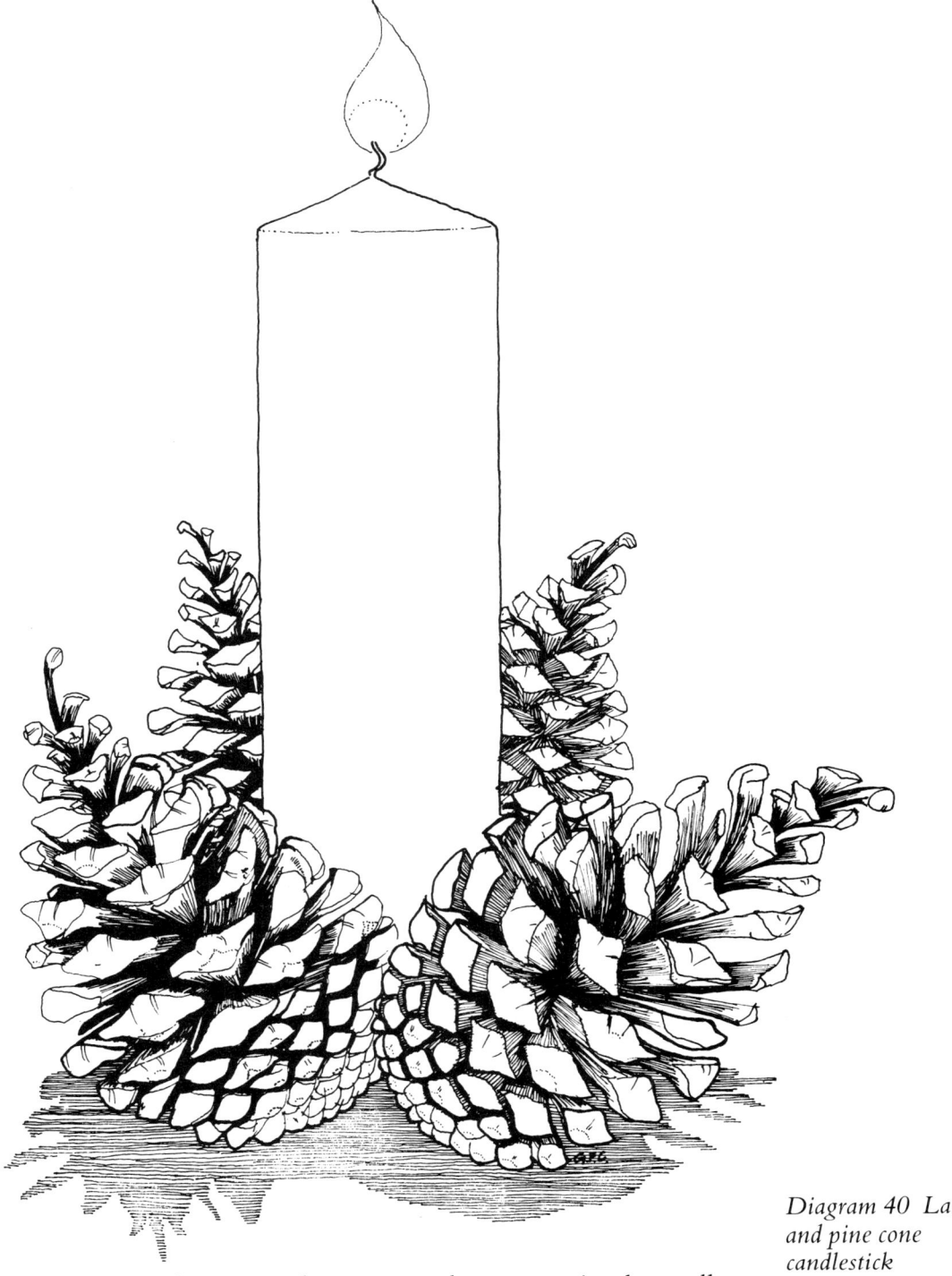

Diagram 40 Larch and pine cone candlestick

Use them in their natural state to make a very simple candle holder which will fit snugly round the base of any size of candle. For small candles use the smaller larch cones to make the holder, for fatter candles use small or medium-sized pine cones.

Candle holders

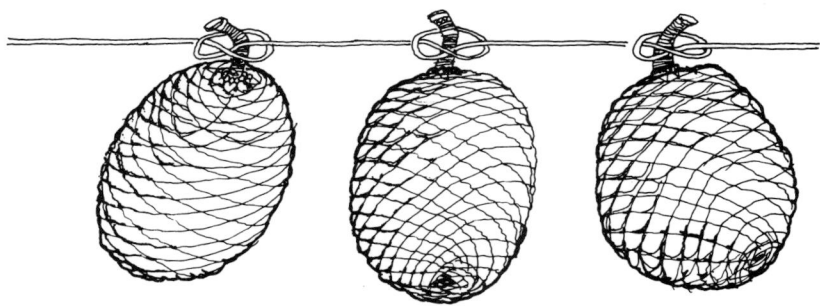

elastic tied around stems of larch cones...

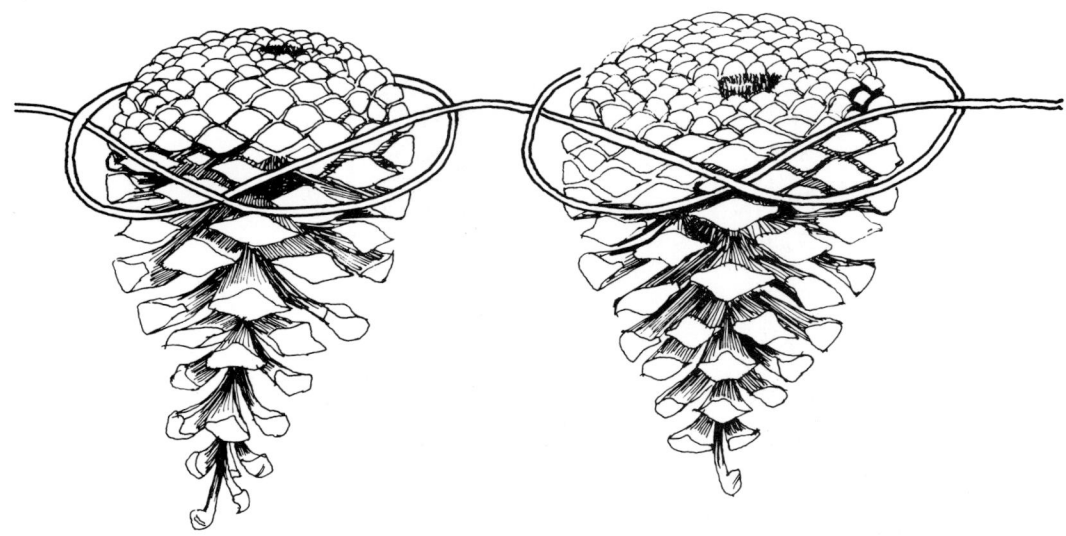

thread elastic around spines of pine cones...

You will need a length of round elastic. A larch cone usually has a small stem at the base of the cone. Knot the elastic round the stems, working with the elastic stretched.

Tie them as closely as possible with the edges of the cones touching so that when the tension on the elastic is released the cones spring back in to a cluster. Knot the two ends of the elastic together to form a circle and slip it over the base of the candle.

The larger pine cone does not usually have a stem attached so the elastic must be threaded through the spines near the base and each cone must be tied on individually.

Keep the sides of the cones touching and the elastic taut. One row of these larger cones is usually enough around the candle base. An attractive centre piece for the Christmas dinner table can quickly be made, by positioning the candle and pine cone holder on the table and adding the tips of branches of fir (the lower branches which usually need to be trimmed from the Christmas tree are ideal for this). Holly or laurel with a few trails of ivy placed in a circle radiating outwards from the cones also looks very pretty. A few Christmas baubles or miniature crackers resting on top of the greenery will add a touch of colour. Another idea is to use gold or silver candles and spray the cones with gold or silver metallic paint.

Making fir cone carollers

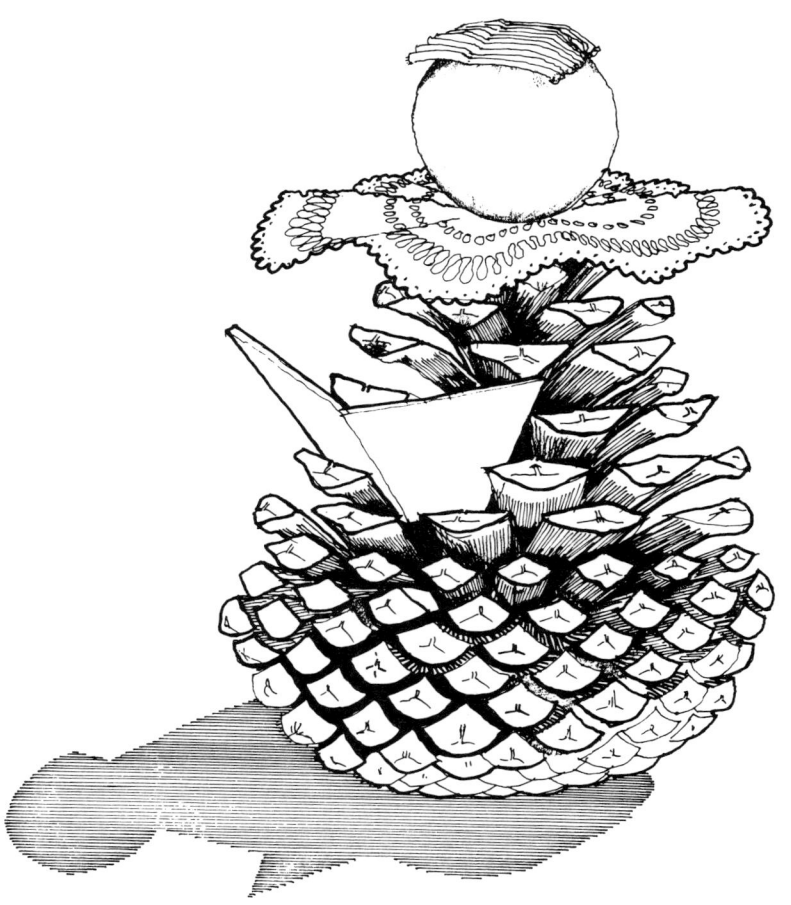

Diagram 41 Fir cone caroller

Fat pine cones make excellent choir boys! (See diagram 41.) To make them, choose chubby cones which are fairly well open. You will also need: Christmas tree baubles about 2.5cm diameter; glue; a

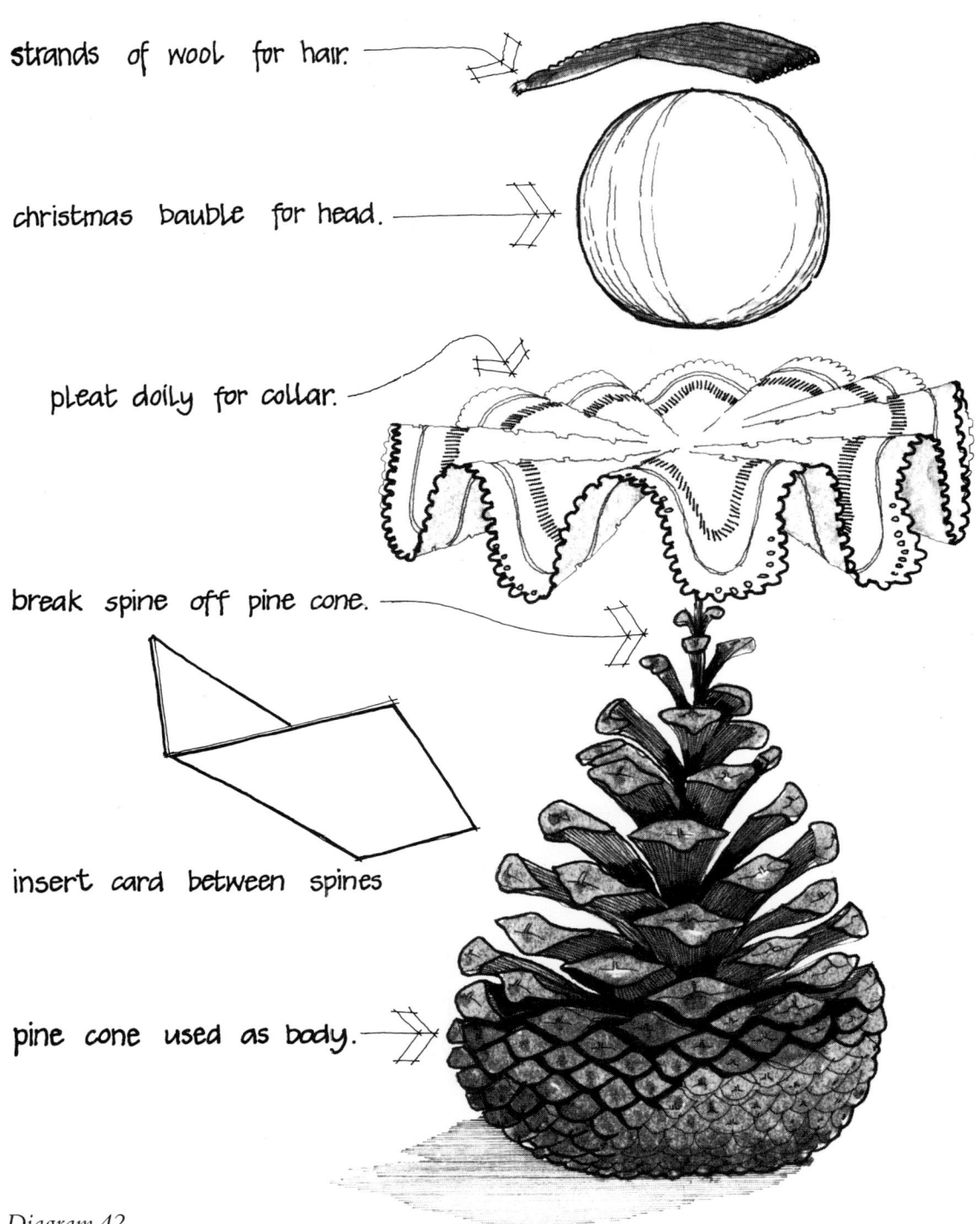

strands of wool for hair.

christmas bauble for head.

pleat doily for collar.

break spine off pine cone.

insert card between spines

pine cone used as body.

Diagram 42

66

white paper doily; thin card; polyfilla or plasticine and scraps of wool.

Remove the metal shank from the bauble. Or if you are using the unbreakable thread–covered baubles, cut off the small hanging loop.

Remove the centre from the cone by breaking off the centre spine, with a twisting movement (so that the bauble can fit into the cone). Stand the cone upright on a base of cardboard, a piece of bark or a small log, fixing it with plasticine or polyfilla.

Cut a strip about 10cm long and 2.5cm wide from the outside edge of the doily. Pleat the strip into a circle. Spread glue over the top of a bauble and glue the paper circle to the bauble. Add a dab of glue to the top of the pine cone, glue the bauble to the cone with the paper between the bauble and the cone, forming a ruffle at the neck (diagram 42).

Cut several strands of wool about 2.5cm long. Spread glue over the top of the bauble and press the wool in place to form hair.

Cut a piece of card about 4cm × 2cm. Fold it in half and insert it between the spines of the cones to make a hymn book for the carol singer.

Children's party
Make a carol singer for each child. Use these as place markers, standing them beside each child's place at the table with their own name written on the hymn book.

Snow scene table centre piece

Select a short branch with a graceful or twisted shape. Brush the edges of the branches and one side of the stem with white emulsion paint or white canvas shoe cleaner to give the impression of a dusting of snow.

Fix the branch at one end of a piece of bark or log using a stiff paste of polyfilla or plasticine to hold it in place. You will need to prop up the branch by some means such as an upturned book until the polyfilla is quite hard. Stand a group of carol singers under the branch, securing them with the plasticine or polyfilla.

Mix a quantity of white 'Tide' washing powder to a thick crumbly paste. Spread this over the log and round the base of the 'tree', leaving the surface rough to give the appearance of drifts of snow. The Tide will dry absolutely hard and last indefinitely . (No other washing powder gives the same results!)

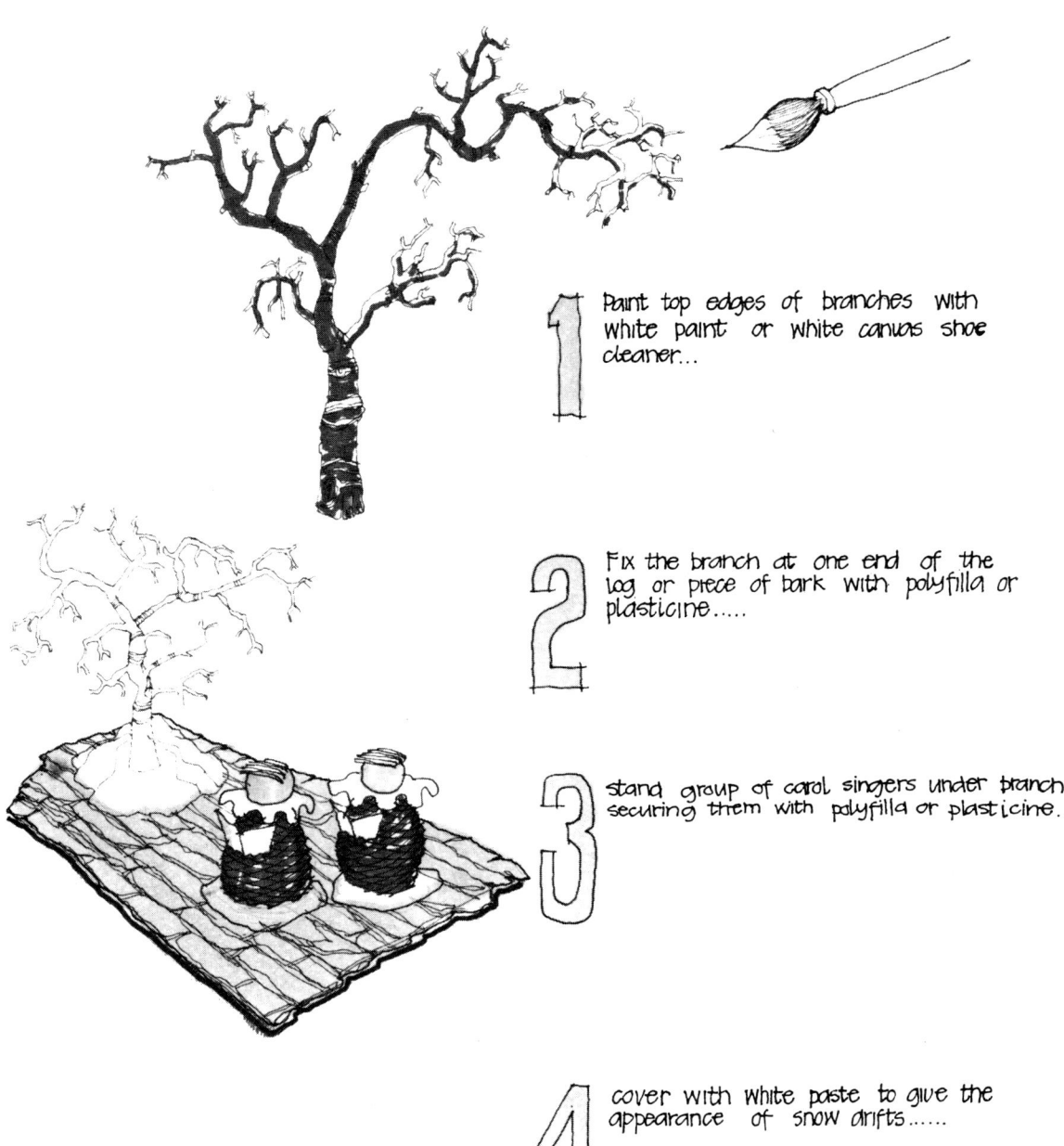

1 Paint top edges of branches with white paint or white canvas shoe cleaner...

2 Fix the branch at one end of the log or piece of bark with polyfilla or plasticine.....

3 Stand group of carol singers under branch, securing them with polyfilla or plasticine.

4 Cover with white paste to give the appearance of snow drifts......

Diagram 43 Snow-scene table centrepiece

Fir cone angel

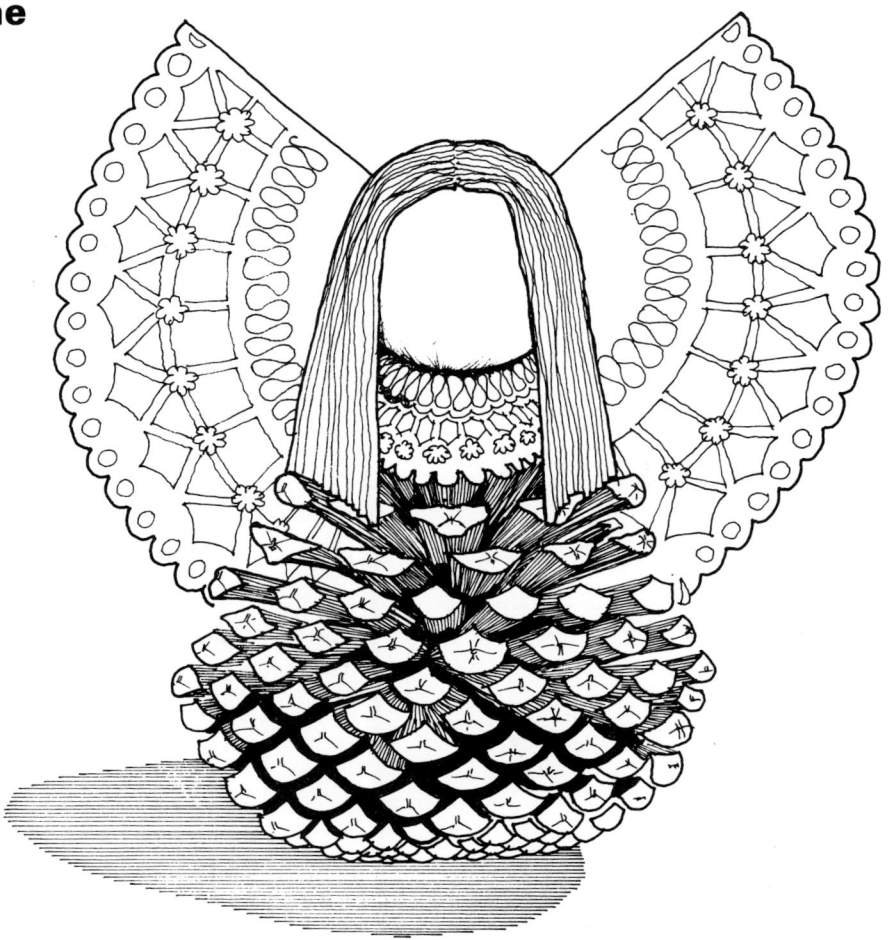

Diagram 44

You will need a very large fir cone – the larger the better; a large gold Christmas bauble (about 6cm diameter), a gold doily, yellow wool for the hair and polyfilla or plasticine.

Follow the instructions given for the fir cone carollers to fix the bauble to the cone, making the ruffle for the neck of the angel from a strip cut from the edge of the gold doily, about 5cm by 25cm. Stand the angel under a gnarled branch fixed to a piece of bark or a log, following the instructions. Brush the base as well as the branch with white emulsion or canvas shoe cleaner.

Cut two large wings from the rest of the gold doily and glue these to the back of the cone. Cut strands of wool about 25cm long. Tie these loosely together at the centre and glue them to the top of the 'head', so that they hang down evenly at the sides (diagram 44).

10 All Sorts of Snowmen

Diagram 45

Comical Snowmen

This family of snowmen is very easy to make (diagram 45). They are simple enough for small children to attempt with the minimum of adult supervision, and they can be made to any size. If you make several snowmen graded in size they look very effective displayed on a flight of stairs, ranging from the smallest snowman on the bottom step to the largest snowman at the top. They also look very decorative placed in a group in an alcove, or at the foot of the Christmas tree.

Materials required

Thin cardboard (old shirt boxes are ideal)
Roll of cheap household cotton wool
Adhesive
Scraps of red and black felt
Sellotape

The snowmen are made up from three cone shapes, and the cones are made from semi-circles of thin card. The diameter of the cone used for the base is approximately 2.5cm larger than the cones for the head and the hat. For example, for the largest snowman, cut one semi-circle of card approximately diameter 32.5cm and two semi-circles of card approximately 30cm diameter.

Since these are only suggested sizes, you can obviously use the handiest size of dinner plate, or pan lid, to draw round the semi-circles as long as you can make the base semi-circle approximately 2.5cm more in diameter than the other two (diagram 46).

TO ASSEMBLE THE CONES
Bend the straight edge of the semi-circle of card in half. Overlap the straight edges about 2.5cm to form a cone. Staple or sellotape the edges to hold them in place.

Cut off the point of the larger base cone to a depth of 2.5cm. Make cuts round the top of the cone about 1cm apart and 1cm deep.

Brush adhesive around the inside of the top of the cone. Insert the point of the second cone. Press it in firmly and allow to dry.

Make cuts around the open top of this second cone, about 1cm apart and 1cm deep. Bend them gently to the inside of the cone.

Unroll the cotton wool. Peel off a strip long enough to wrap round the cones and overlap, and wide enough to cover the two cones, plus about 2.5cm. Brush the surface and inside rim at the top and base of the cones with adhesive. Press the cotton wool over the cones, tucking the extra fabric inside the cone at the top and bottom. Ease in the cotton wool at the neck of the figure

Cover the third cone for the hat with cotton wool in the same way. Press it firmly on to the body. Glue a small ball of cotton wool to the top of the hat.

Tie a strip of red felt or fabric round the neck for a scarf. Add

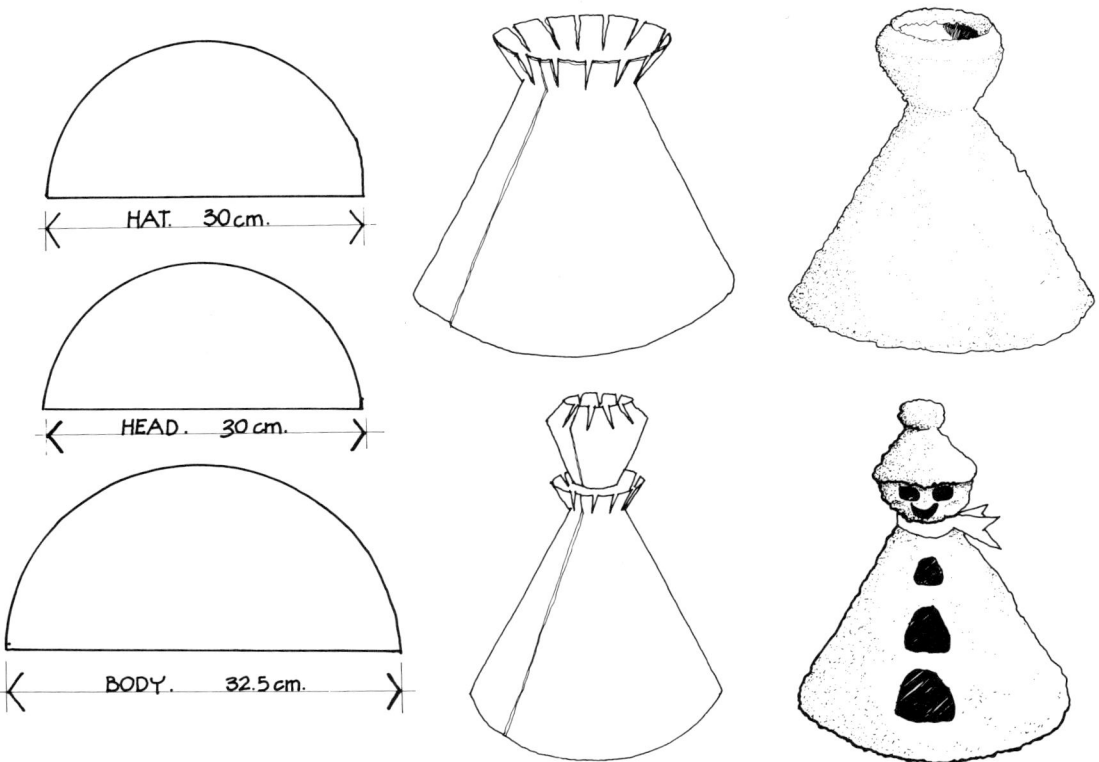

circles of black fabric for buttons and eyes, and a small crescent shape for the mouth.

Diagram 46

Make several snowmen grading them evenly in size. The smallest snowman in the illustration was cut from a semi-circle with a diameter of 15cm for the base and 13cm for the head and hat.

Snowmen containers

These super snowmen are made from empty cylindrical cartons with lids (diagram 48). The smallest sizes are made from empty spice tubs filled with small sweets, such as jelly babies and dolly mixtures. Intermediate sizes can be made from empty coffee jars filled with assorted toffees and the largest snowman is made from the biggest round container with a lid that you can find (such as catering sizes of coffee or dishwashing powder). The large snowman can be filled with lollipops or toffee apples and is also ideal for use as a lucky dip, filled with small wrapped gifts for a children's party.

Since the hats of these snowmen are removable to reveal the contents, they must be able to withstand quite a bit of handling and

Diagram 47 Snowmen containers need to be made of something more durable than the cotton wool used for the comical snowmen. Thick white cellulose wadding, of the kind used for quilting is ideal. It is soft and fluffy in appearance and relatively cheap. It is available from fabric departments. You will also need adhesive, scraps of red and black felt and suitable contents for the snowman.

TO ASSEMBLE THE SNOWMEN
Cut a strip of thick wadding to the depth of the container and long enough to wrap round the outside and overlap by 2.5cm. (Thin wadding can be used double.) Smear glue over the surface of the container and press the wadding to the sides. Glue at the join.

Cut a second strip of wadding the same size. Join the two short sides at one end only. You can use glue or several firm backstitches to join the wadding.

This forms the brim of the hat. Pull this closed end of the hat over the top of the snowman. Gather up the fabric tightly about half way down its length into a white elastic band or white rolled elastic.

Bend the fabric over at the top to form a bobble for the hat and tuck the ends underneath the elastic.

Glue semi-circles of black felt, peeping out from underneath the hat, for the eyes and a small red felt circle for the nose. Cut a scarf from a soft red fabric and tie it round the snowman about one third of the way down, leaving plenty of room to glue black fabric or felt buttons in place.

Remove the hat and fill the snowman with sweets, lollipops or small wrapped gifts. Replace the container lid, or, if the lid is not suitable, press crumpled tissue paper over the filling to hold it. Replace the hat, at a slight angle, and turn it back on itself at the base for about 2.5cm to form a brim.

Diagram 48

11 Nativity Scene

Diagram 49   Christmas would be incomplete without a Nativity scene, it is, however, one of the most difficult things to make. All too often a Nativity scene can end up looking decidedly scrappy and cheap. On the other hand, ready-made plaster images or plastic dolls can be very unattractive, and to some people almost offensive.

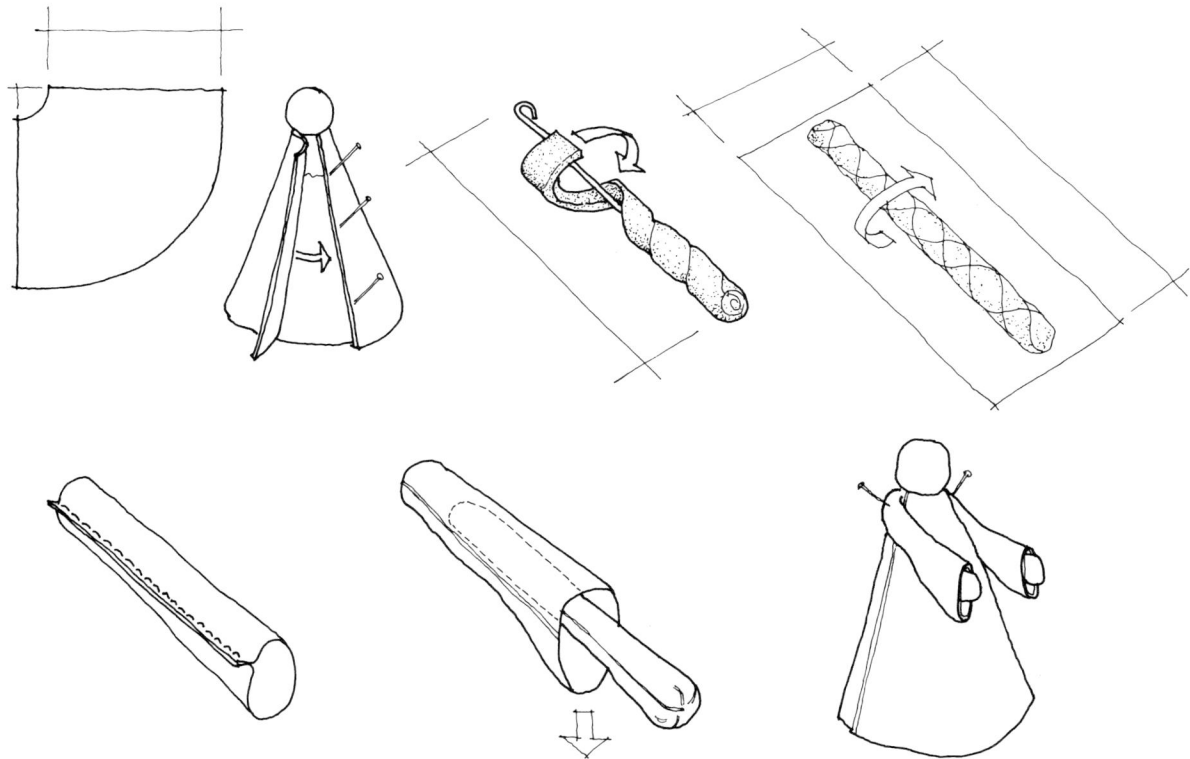

A happy compromise lies in using natural materials such as *Diagram 50* hessian, and making stylised figures which suggest faces and features rather than defining them. A suggestion of movement can be introduced by the angle of a head or an out-stretched arm.

This Nativity scene has been made entirely in different coloured hessian. Hessian, particularly when it is cut on the cross is a very pliable fabric which drapes well. It is extremely easy to work with and can be shaped and moulded and has sufficient body to keep the shape it is given. It is also relatively cheap and available in a wide range of muted colours from craft or embroidery shops.

Try making the central figures of the Nativity scene, Mary and Joseph, in natural hessian first. Once you have worked with the fabric and realise how readily it adapts itself into pleasing curves and holds these lines, you can then create other figures for yourself, or follow these instructions for three kings and two shepherds.

The base of the figure is made from a sturdy cardboard cone, approximately 18cm high and diameter 7cm at the base. The inside of a cone of wool is ideal, or make the cones from a semi-circle of card, diameter 36cm. (Bend the card half way along the straight side and overlap these straight edges to form a cone. Staple or glue the edges together.)

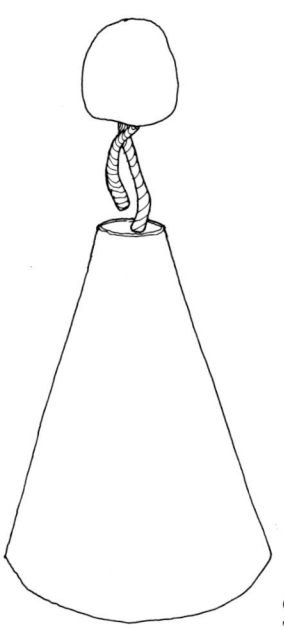

Diagram 51

The heads are made from cotton waste balls – the kind sold for dolls heads – and are available from craft or embroidery shops. These are preferable to wooden balls, as the soft cotton can be pierced so that the head can be held at an angle.

The arms are simply made from wire, covered first with cotton wool and then with hessian. Not all the figures need arms but they take way the stiffness of the cone shape and they can bend as you like to adopt different poses.

Very little sewing is needed to make the figures. The edges of the fabric are not neatened and the clothing is held firmly in place with pins and adhesive.

Materials required

THE FIGURES

Mary and Joseph 50cm natural hessian 90cm wide, a scrap of blue hessian
1st King 20cm orange hessian 90cm wide
2nd King 20cm dull gold hessian 90cm wide
3rd King 20cm maroon hessian 90cm wide
The two shepherds 50cm green hessian 90cm wide
2 packets of pipe cleaners
7 cotton waste balls (4–5cm diameter) from craft or embroidery shops
7 sturdy cardboard cones approximately 15cm high with the base approximately 6cm diameter
Soft wire or florists' stem wire for the arms
Pins and adhesive
Cotton wool

Diagram 52 Joseph

JOSEPH

Enlarge the small hole in the cotton ball with the point of a knife. Bend a pipe cleaner in two. Dab adhesive at the looped end of the pipe cleaner. Press this end firmly into the hole in the ball.

Dab adhesive round the point of the cone. Insert the other two ends of the pipe cleaner into the cone. Press the head onto the cone and allow to dry.

Covering the head

Cut a 15cm square of hessian on the cross, i.e. cut diagonally across the grain of the fabric.

Cover the head with the hessian, ease it in at the neck by winding a strong thread several times round the neck. Adjust the fullness to leave one side as free as possible of folds or pleats. (This will be the face.) Tie off the ends of the thread.

Covering the cone

Cut a quarter-circle of fabric with the straight sides the same as the height of the cone. Scoop out a slight curve at the point.

Wrap this around the figure, with the scooped out curve at the neck concealing the raw edges of the hessian which covers the head. Overlap the fabric at the back. Trim off the surplus fabric at the back and at the base so that the cone is neatly covered. Fasten the back seam with dabs of glue and by pushing several pins vertically through the fabric to the inside of the cone.

Making the arms and sleeves

Cut a length of wire 26cm long. Wrap the wire in a layer of cotton wool and bind with thread to hold it in place (diagram 50).

Cut a strip of hessian on the cross, 30cm ×6cm. Wrap the covered wire in the hessian, turn in the ends and the raw edges and oversew the long sides together.

Cut a strip of hessian on the cross 30cm × 9cm. Fold it in half lengthwise. Stitch the long sides together, taking a narrow 3-4mm seam. (This can be done by machine.) Turn the strip right side out. Insert the arms into this tube of fabric, which forms the sleeves. Turn under about 2cm of the fabric at each end, pulling the edge slightly so that it forms a wide edge to the sleeve.

Attach the arms to the figure at the back of the neck with concealed pins and dabs of adhesive. Bend the arms forwards and downwards.

To complete Joseph

Cut a strip of fabric, on the cross, 20cm × 6cm. Drape this over the head to hang down at the sides. Hold in place with pins pushed through the hessian into the head. Fray out several strands of hessian and tie in a band over the top of the head, concealing the pins.

MARY

Cut off the base of the cone to reduce the height to 10cm. Attach the head to the body as with Joseph, but position the head at a forward angle, so that the finished figure appears to be looking down.

Cover the head as before. Cut a strip of fabric on the cross, 35cm × 16cm. Stitch the short sides together. Turn the fabric right side out. Using a strong thread work a row of running stitches along one side of the fabric about 1cm from the edges. Ease up the fabric into gathers, to form the skirt.

Covering the cone

Slip it over the cone. Ease the fabric up to fit the cone at the waist. Hold in place with pins pressed through the fabric vertically into the cone. Cut a cross cut strip of hessian 4cm × 16cm. Wrap this round the top of the cone to form the bodice of the dress and to conceal the raw edges at the neck and waist. Overlap the fabric at the back and secure with pins and adhesive.

Cut a section from the discarded base of the cone 3cm deep. Seat the figure on this, spreading the skirt to the front. Secure with adhesive and pins.

Make arms and sleeves and attach them to the body, following the instructions given for Joseph. Bend the arms forwards, and the

Diagram 53 Mary

right arm lower than the left. Make a small ball from a piece of cotton wool covered with a circle of hessian to represent the baby's head. Wrap this in a scrap of hessian, winding it round to resemble a shawl. Place the baby in Mary's right arm, holding it in place invisibly with pins.

To complete Mary
Cut a strip of royal blue hessian 18cm × 6cm. Fold back 1cm along one long side. Cut the short sides obliquely.

Drape this over the head with the turned-back edge to the front. Hold in place with pins pushed into the head and concealed under the turned edge.

The other figures are made in the same way with slight variations in their dress.

Diagram 54 The shepherds

FIRST SHEPHERD

Make a slanting cut, removing a section about 1cm deep at one side, from the base of the cone.

This will make the figure lean slightly forward. Attach the head, bending the pipe cleaner, so that the head tilts forward also. Cut a strip of green hessian, on the cross, the circumference of the cone plus 3cm and 13cm wide. Join the short sides and turn the fabric right side out. Slip it over the cone and ease it in at the neck. Hold in place with pins pushed through into the cardboard. Bind round with thread to secure firmly.

Make and attach the arms. Cut a strip of hessian on the cross. Drape it round the neck and over the arms, to conceal the raw edges of the fabric, pinning invisibly in place at the front.

Cover the head and add a girdle following the instructions for Joseph.

SECOND SHEPHERD

The cone is not trimmed down for this shepherd and the head is attached vertically, as for Joseph. Follow the directions given for the first shepherd, but cover the head with a cross-cut strip of hessian, tying it in at the neck to resemble a hood. Make a shepherd's crook from a pipe cleaner, and hold it in place with a dab of glue.

Diagram 55 The kings

FIRST KING

This figure has no arms and a full length cloak. Shorten a cone by
2.5cm at the base and make this cut slightly at an angle. Cover the
cone with gold hessian and attach and cover the head as for Joseph.
Cut a circle of gold hessian approximately 20cm diameter for the
cloak. Fold down about 4cm at one edge, to form a collar. Wrap the
cloak round the body overlapping it at the front. Hold it in place
invisibly with pins. Cut a strip of hessian 5cm wide and long
enough to wrap round the head and overlap. Cut it into deep points
along one edge. Pin round the head to form the crown.

SECOND KING

This figure has no arms and a short cloak. Cover the cone with
maroon hessian and attach and cover the head as for Joseph. Cut a
circle of hessian 15cm diameter for the cloak (draw round a saucer).
Fold down about 2.5cm at one edge to form a collar. Pin the cloak to
the body under the collar at the back of the neck and sides only,
leaving the front edge clear of the body.

Cut a strip of of hessian 5cm wide and long enough to go round
the head and overlap. Turn back 1cm along one long edge. With
this folded edge forming a brim, wrap the strip round the head and
hold in place invisibly with pins.

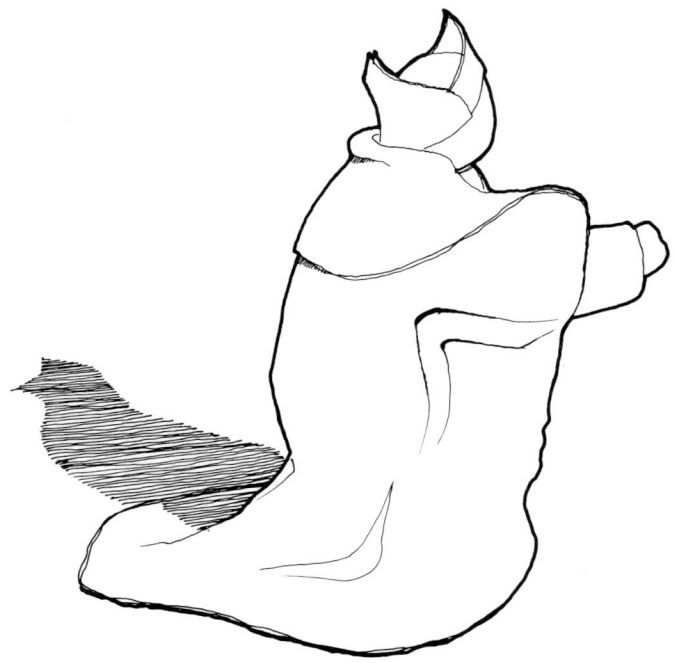

KNEELING KING

Reduce a cone with a slanting cut to about 10cm in height. Attach head at a forward angle and cover the cone as for Joseph. Make arms and attach these invisibly with pins. Bend the wire so that the arms stretch forwards.

Cut a circle approximately 20cm for the cape. Fold back one edge about 1cm and pin the cape to the back of the neck, under the fold. Pin it invisibly to the sides of the body.

Cut a strip of hessian 5cm deep and long enough to wrap round the head and overlap. Wrap it round the head and pin invisibly in place. Cut out a deep V-shape at each side to resemble a mitre.

TO ASSEMBLE THE NATIVITY SCENE

You may have just the right alcove or bookshelves in which to display the figures, in which case you can group them according to your own ideas. But if you want to make a backdrop to display the figures, here is one simple suggestion.

A wooden fruit box, with a slatted floor – the kind that also has strips of wood at each side for handles makes an ideal backing for the scene. Paint the box with a dark wood stain. When it is dry stand it on its side and tie strips of bark to the handles at each end. Place a long piece of bark on top for the roof, extending over the ends. Arrange the figures as shown and sprinkle short ends of straw on the floor around the figures.

12 Party Paper Flowers

These enormous tissue paper flowers are very simple to make and create a bold splash of colour for a party. They look very effective arranged in a garden tub wired on to branches of real greenery such as laurel or fir. They can also be wired on to a real houseplant such as a large rubber plant. For a Christmas display wire them to branches of holly and spray the whole arrangement with a can of Christmas snow.

Diagram 56

Materials required

Packets of tissue paper in assorted colours
Florists' stem wire
Branches of greenery

Construction

Cut the tissue paper to give twelve layers measuring 25cm / 36cm approximately. Place the layers of paper in a pile on the table with their edges together and the shorter side towards you. Beginning at your side, and keeping all the layers together, fold the paper across the width, forming accordion pleats each about 2.5cm deep.

Grip the pleated paper with one hand and with the other bend the wire round the pleats at the *centre* of the strip, twisting the wire back on itself to hold the pleated paper firmly. Now hold the wire stem between your knees, or get someone to hold it for you to leave both hands free. Gently pull out the top layer of tissue each side of the centre, working at the outer edges, until it points upwards. Pull the next layer upwards to lie about 2.5cm away from the first layer. Continue in this way until by the fifth layer you have formed a flower head. Pull the bottom layer to point downwards, and continue until you have separated all the layers and formed a perfect ball-shaped flower, which you can wire to the end of one of the branches.

Arrange the flowers in a large container, remembering to add water to keep the greenery fresh.

Diagram 57

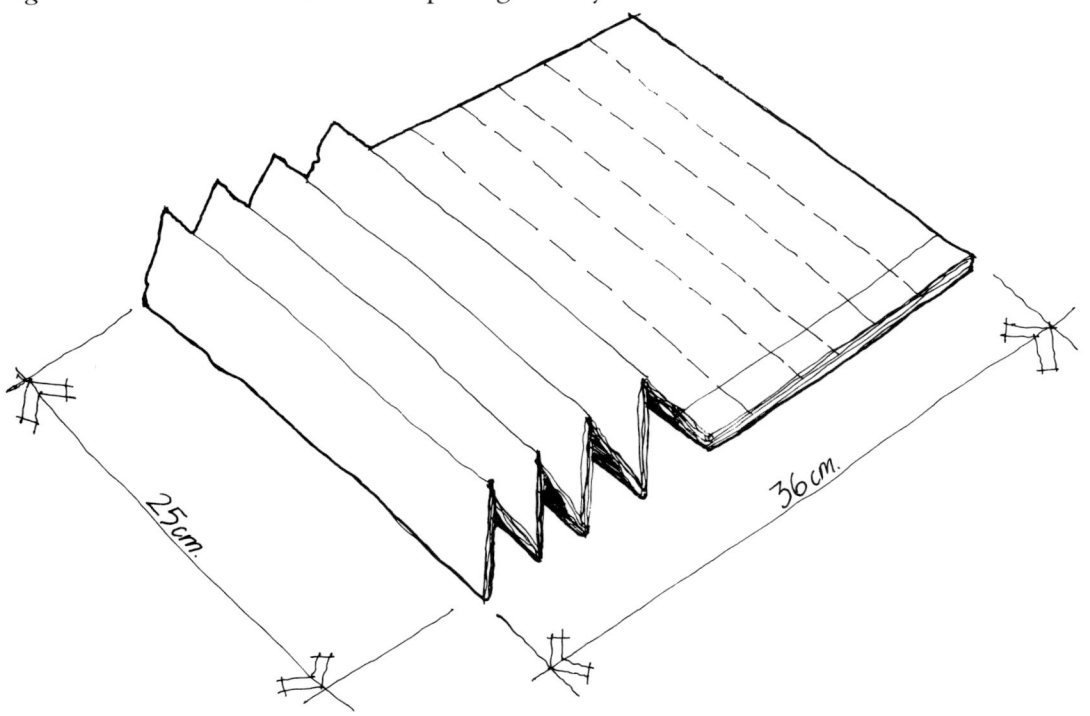

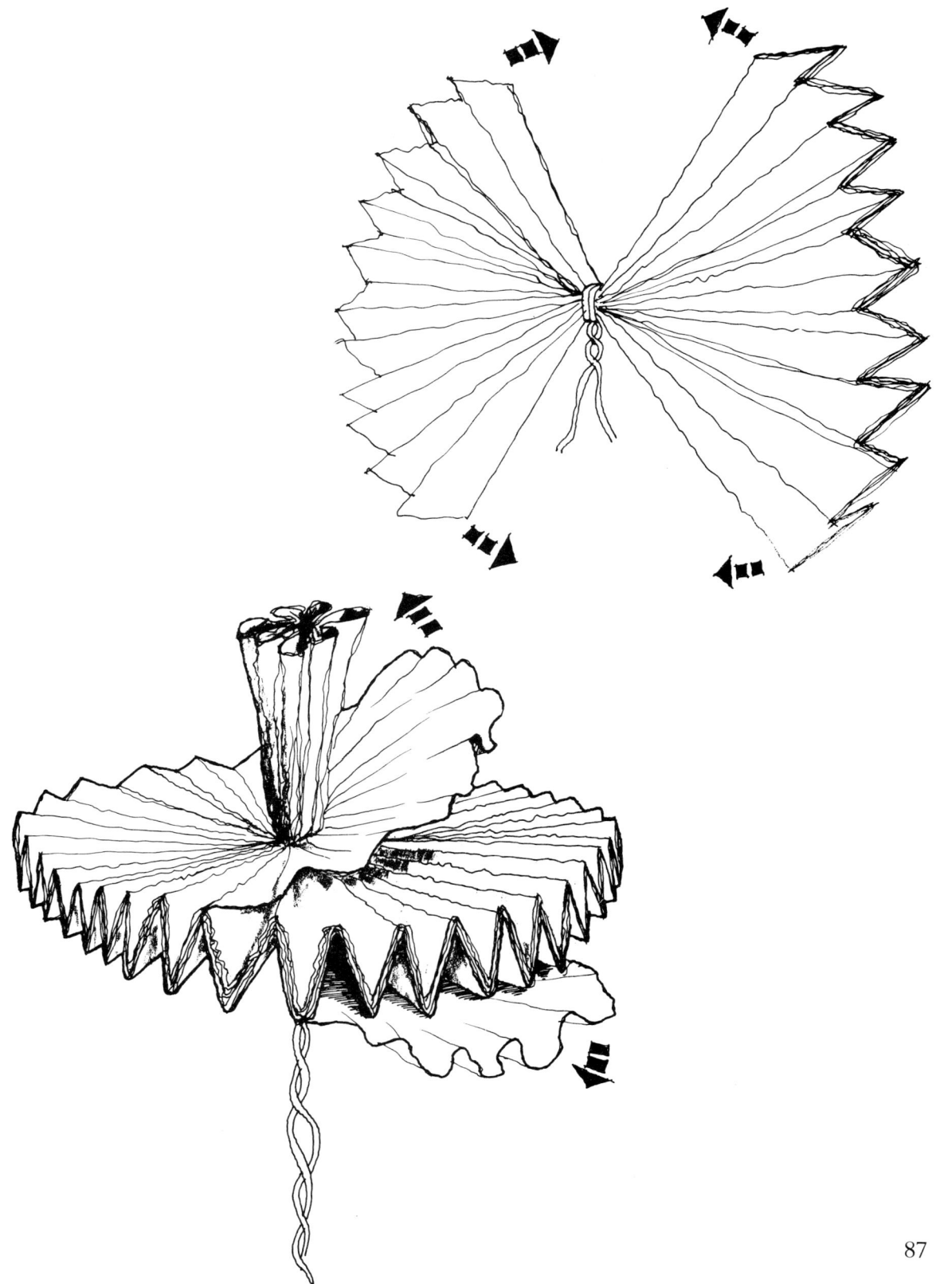

13
Supper Table Centrepiece

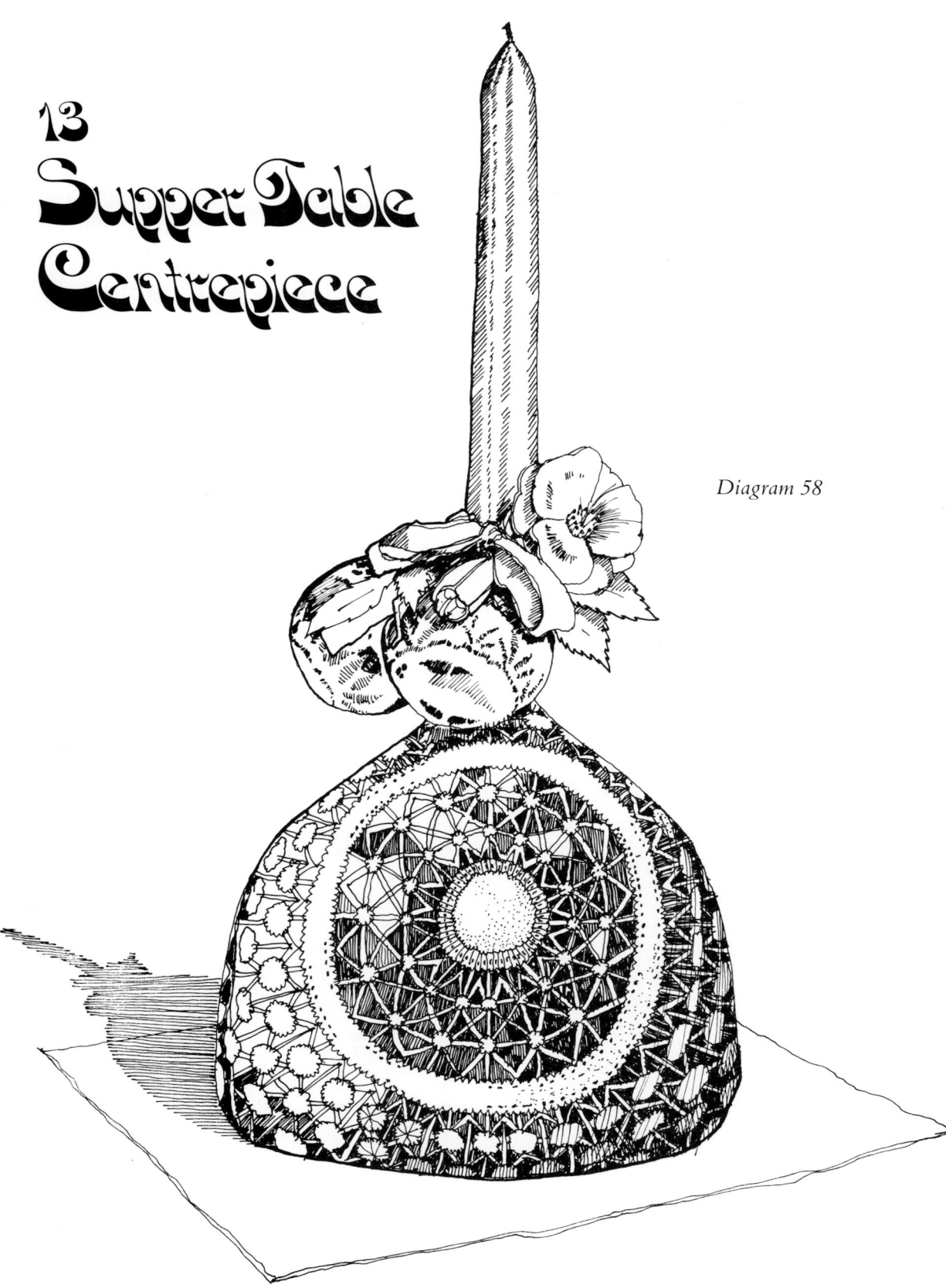

Diagram 58

Flowers are the ideal centrepiece for any supper party but when they are in short supply gleaming bottle and candle decorations are an excellent substitute. They will supplement the flowers for a wedding party, and make an ideal focal point for a Christmas buffet supper or an inexpensive gift for a friend.

The base of the arrangement is an empty, nicely shaped bottle such as a Mateus Rose or Courvoisier brandy bottle. This is covered with a silver or gold doily, and the neck of the bottle is decorated appropriately below the candle. You will need several of these candle decorations, one for each table at a large function, or grouped at intervals on a long buffet table.

WEDDING ARRANGEMENT

Materials required

1 packet of silver doilys (large size)
Clear-drying craft glue
90cm white double-edged satin ribbon (5cm wide)
80cm Tootals silver ribbon (2cm wide)
Florists wire
2 artificial white carnations
1 silver fern or leaf
1 silver or white candle, 20cm long

COVERING THE BOTTLE

First, look at the doily and work out the best way to use the design on the doily. The simplest way is to use two doilys, one for the back of the bottle, and one for the front and overlap them at the sides. Cut out the shape of half the bottle in paper first, lying the bottle flat on the paper and drawing round the outline. Place the doily over this paper shape to give you an idea of how the finished design will look. When you cut the shape from the silver doily remember to allow 1cm extra at the edges for the overlap.

Brush the surface of the bottle with adhesive. A flat pastry brush is ideal for this. Press the doily to the sides of the bottles, easing it gently round the bottle neck. Brush the surface again with adhesive, especially at the joins. Allow several hours to dry.

Pare down the base of the candle so that it fits the neck of the bottle.

Tie the satin ribbon in a bow. Tie the silver ribbon into a slightly smaller bow and place over the white bow. Wire the bows together at the centre and then twist the wire around the bottle neck.

Wire the carnations and silver leaf together and wire these on top of the bows and around the bottle neck. Cut the ends of the ribbons as shown in diagram 59.

Diagram 59

CHRISTMAS ARRANGEMENT

1 packet gold doilys (large size)
Clear-drying craft glue
Gold candle, 20cm long
2 large gold Christmas baubles
A spray of artificial Christmas roses or greenery (holly)
50cm gold ribbon

Cover the bottle with the gold doilys as above. Wire the baubles together and hang them round the neck of the bottle. Tie the ribbon into a bow. Wire this above the baubles and wire the Christmas greenery on top of the bow.

Smaller bottles also look good covered with the gold doily and using only a looped bow of gold ribbon at the neck and a smaller gold candle.

Conversion Table

METRIC CONVERSION CHART (approximate)

cm	in	g	oz
0.5	3/16	3.5	1/2
1	3/8	6.5	1
2	3/4	13.5	2
3	1 1/8	27.5	4
4	1 5/8	55	8
5	2	110	16
6	2 3/8	220	32
7	2 3/4	440	64
8	3 1/8		
9	3 1/2		
10	4		
20	7 7/8		
30	11 7/8		
40	15 3/4		
50	19 5/8		
100	39 3/8		

Suppliers

CHRISTMAS CRACKER KITS AND COMPONENT PARTS
The Craft Centre
Claremont Street
Aberdeen

The Handicraft Shop
47 Northgate
Canterbury
Kent

FUR FABRICS AND TOY FILLINGS
Granary Crafts
Bookham
Surrey
(Furmofelt stockist)

Fluffy Fabrics
Unit N1/N2 Tribune Drive
Trinity Trading Estate
Sittingbourne
Kent

Oakley Fabrics Ltd
60 Collingdon Street
Luton
Beds.

Saflon Ltd
Saffron Way
LE2 6UP

And branches of John Lewis who also stock plastic safety eyes and noses

FELT AND HESSIAN
The Felt and Hessian Shop
Dept SK 12
34 Greville Street
London EC1

DRESS FABRICS
Aitkens of North Berwick Ltd
93 High Street
North Berwick
East Lothian

John Lewis Partnership
Oxford Street
London W1 (and branches)

The Fabric Studio
10 Frith Street
London W1

Further Reading

Anderson, E. *The Technique of Soft Toy Making*, Batsford 1982
Anderson, E. *Patterns for Soft Toys*, Batsford, 1985
Mochrie, E., and Roseaman, I.P., *Cut Woolly Toys*, Dryad, 1979
Mochrie, E., and Roseaman, I.P., *Felt Toys*, Dryad, 1979
Snook, B., *Creative Soft Toys*, Dryad, 1985
Snook, B., *Embroidery Stitches*, Dryad, 1985
Snook, B., *Learning to Sew*, Dryad, 1985
Walker, D., *Making Doll's Clothes*, Batsford 1980